POSTMODERNISM AND THE NEW ENLIGHTENMENT

HUGO A. MEYNELL

POSTMODERNISM AND THE NEW ENLIGHTENMENT

The Catholic University of America Press
Washington, D.C.

Printed in the United States of America
The paper used in this publication meets the minimum requirements of American National Standards for Information Science—Permanence of Paper for Printed Library materials ANSI A39.48-1984.

LIBRARY OF CONGRESS CATALOGING-IN-PUBLICATION DATA

Meynell, Hugo Anthony.
Postmodernism and the New Enlightenment / by Hugo A. Meynell.
p. cm.
Includes bibliographical references and index.
1. Postmodernism. I. Title.
B831.2.M48 1999
149′.97—dc21
99-17999
ISBN 0-8132-0946-3 (cloth : alk. paper).
ISBN 0-8132-0947-1 (pbk. : alk. paper)

For Shadia Drury

whom it is not permitted for the base
even to praise

A civilization in decline digs its own grave
with a relentless consistency

(Bernard Lonergan, *Method in Theology*)

Sometimes I go about and poison wells

(Christopher Marlowe, *The Jew of Malta*)

"The garbage man's arrived." "Tell him we
don't want any."

(The Marx Brothers)

CONTENTS

PREFACE AND ACKNOWLEDGMENTS

When I was asked to give a series of lectures on postmodernism at the University of Lethbridge in 1995, I had already been both intrigued and exasperated by the phenomenon for several years. I was especially provoked by the habit in authors called postmodernist of attacking "obscenely and courageously" (as Bottom put it) the reason characteristic of the Enlightenment. The lectures were never delivered, due to lack of subscribers; but in the notes that I had prepared for them, there seemed to me to be the makings of a short book on the subject.

What I want to argue in this book may conveniently be summarized as follows:

1. The "New Enlightenment" may be envisaged as a synthesis of Enlightenment thesis and postmodernist antithesis.[1]

2. There are two aspects of Nietzsche's thought; one leading to nihilism, both moral and cognitive, by way of postmodernism; the other to human authenticity as conceived by the New Enlightenment.

3. The essence of the New Enlightenment is an account of truth and value determined by four "transcendental precepts": "be attentive, be intelligent, be reasonable, be responsible" (Lonergan). These may be justified by the fact that their alternatives are self-destructive.

4. One may be attentive to one's own feelings, or indeed

1. So far as I know, the term 'New Enlightenment' was first coined, and applied to the work of Bernard Lonergan, by Professor Fred Lawrence, in conversation.

to one's mental acts, as well as to the sense experiences that are the staple of empiricism as usually conceived.

5. Intelligence is a matter of envisaging possibilities and hypothesizing in response to the questions "What?" and "Why?"; reasonableness of affirming in each case—definitely or provisionally as is appropriate—the hypothesis that best fits the evidence (as opposed to what happens to soothe our fears, gratify our self-esteem, justify the privileges of ourselves or our groups, etc.).

6. One can come to reasonable judgments about what is good or bad as well as true or false; to be responsible is to act in accordance with such judgments.

7. Nietzsche and his postmodernist successors are often splendidly subversive of judgments that are less than fully reasonable, and of decisions that are by no means responsible but pretend to be so. Foucault's "genealogies" in particular bring out how far apparently descriptive or explanatory discourse about insanity, criminality, sexuality, and so on, is in fact largely a device for control and the exercise of power by some people over others.

8. But unless what is stated by postmodernists themselves amounts to more than mere impositions of power that run counter to ones that have been previously established, there is no reason to take it seriously. How it can is impossible to show in terms countenanced by postmodernists themselves, but can easily be brought out in terms of the New Enlightenment. Postmodernists are to be believed so far as their judgments are more reasonable, more in accordance with the relevant evidence to which one may attend, than those which they are concerned to dispute.

9. If what we may call the Old Enlightenment constitutes the Apollonian, postmodernism contributes the Dionysian, element in the New Enlightenment. The two tendencies may be reconciled in a higher synthesis if one conceives of what is

really true and good in a second-order way, as what is to be known and acted on so far as one resolutely pursues the transcendental precepts rather than being content with "truth" and "goodness" as envisaged here and now. There is always more evidence to which to attend, more possibilities to be envisaged, more individual and social bias to be overcome; and judgments of fact and value will change accordingly.

10. One needs to attend to "subjugated" conceptions of the true and good in as far as those who espouse them are liable to have attended to evidence, and envisaged possibilities, which the conventional and powerful have overlooked.

Roughly, I think a writer is "postmodernist" so far as she repudiates the norms of cognition and evaluation that were propounded and applied by thinkers of the Old Enlightenment, and inveighs against the abuses to which they may be supposed to have given rise. The "New Enlightenment," which is represented above all by the work of Bernard Lonergan, clarifies, modifies, justifies, and applies these norms in such a way that the objections of the postmodernists to Enlightenment rationality are to some extent corroborated, to some extent undercut; but the New Enlightenment firmly and consistently rejects the nihilism and relativism to which postmodernism tends.

An earlier version of the first chapter appeared in New Blackfriars (January 1995). It is reprinted here by kind permission of the editor of that journal.

My thanks are due to many people. I have derived an enormous amount of instruction, stimulus, and encouragement from the conversation and writings of Shadia Drury, and have learned almost as much from my daughter Letitia Meynell. I must thank Ronald Bond, whose administrative measures in effect gave me seven months' extra sabbatical. I also owe a very great debt to a number of my colleagues, too many to mention by name, who have taken the trouble to stand up on my behalf. It is not too much to say that I owe my professional survival, and perhaps my sanity, to their moral and practical support through a time of considerable anxiety and emotional pain. And it is no mere flourish, in my own case, to say how much I owe my wife Jenny, both emotionally and intellectually. Finally, I have to thank Susan Needham, of the Catholic University of America Press, for the improvement of many details and the excision of some infelicities.

POSTMODERNISM AND THE NEW ENLIGHTENMENT

I

NIETZSCHE THE FORERUNNER

FOR ALL THE vast and apparently ever-increasing influence of Friedrich Nietzsche, the precise bearing and implications of his thought remain obscure. I believe that there are two main reasons for this. The first is his poetic, rhapsodic, and gnomic form of self-expression, and his use of language in a manner which makes it seem almost tactless to look for a single, real or precise meaning in what he is saying. (The "exact meaning" of Blake's poem *The Tyger,* I take it, would universally be admitted to be the object of a fool's errand.) The second and, I believe, more important reason is that, so far as unequivocal theoretical and practical consequences can be drawn from what Nietzsche writes, they tend in (at least) two very different directions. To put the matter in another way, there are two quite different paths forward from his thought. One is toward nihilism, in the sense of dissolution of all cognitive and evaluative norms; the other is toward the radical authenticity of what I shall call the New Enlightenment, in which the norms proper to the search for the true and the good are once and for all clearly established. At the end of the first path is a total cognitive and moral chaos where there is no truth, not even the truth that there is no truth, and no good, not even the recognition and implementation of the judgment that there is no good. The second path passes through the fires of a comprehensively radical criticism to find the real ground of rationality and morality, so that the quest for knowledge of what is true and implementation of what is good is put on a firm basis. On the radically sceptical interpretation, Nietzsche was using reason and morality to destroy themselves; on the other account, he was using them rather to clarify their own norms. Which of these two tendencies represents the "real" Nietzsche is, I believe, an unanswerable question; which is the more useful, the one the implications of which are more worth following up and applying, is by no means so, as I shall try to show.

I think that the parable in *Zarathustra* of the camel, the lion, and the child,[1] has an important bearing on this matter. The camel puts up with traditional moral judgments, however burdensome or inimical to life they may be; the lion is indescriminately destructive of all the constraints that the camel had endured. Once the lion has completed its destructive work, one can come with the innocence of childhood to the task of setting up new and more appropriate values, values more favorable to life, on the ruins of the old. One might in a way render Nietzsche's thought consistent by assigning its destructive element to the stage of the lion and its creative aspect to that of the child. Only one who has reduced to utter rubble the ancient and unsanitary building constituted by human morality and traditional custom, Nietzsche seems to be saying, is in a position to build something more useful and commodious for the future.

It has been said that a primary object of Nietzsche's work was "to break down all the concepts and qualities in which

1. F. Nietzsche, *Thus Spoke Zarathustra,* trans. Walter Kaufmann (Harmondsworth: Penguin Books, 1978), 26–27. Subsequent references to *Zarathustra* will be to this edition. As often in Nietzsche, there is an interesting parallel here with William Blake, who distinguished "three classes of men,"

mankind takes pride or pleasure into a few simple qualities in which no one takes pride or pleasure and to see in the latter the origin of the former; likewise to undermine morality by showing its irrational basis."[2] But, one may ask, is the "exposure" itself rational? In that case there is presupposed a sort of rationality that is not reducible to its supposedly irrational basis. But if the exposure is *not* rational, what is the point of taking it seriously? Is not a scepticism that would thus undermine reason self-destructive? How could it possibly be rational or moral to overturn rationality and morality as such? And what would an overturning that was not rational or moral really amount to? It is only on the assumption that, so far from being an actual critique of rationality and morality as such, it is a *genuinely* rational and moral critique of merely *alleged* rationality and morality, that what Nietzsche has to say in this connection can be taken seriously. But *as* thus interpreted, he ought in my opinion to be taken very seriously indeed. Nothing could be more important for civilization than to bring out the differences between true rationality and morality on the one hand, and the very different motives, attitudes, and agendas that have been confused with them on the other. The royal road to what I have called the New Enlightenment is to ask, what sort of criticism it is that destroys itself rather than whatever it purports to be criticizing? And what is to be learned from the fact that it does so? What rational or moral assumptions are implicit in all criticism, and how, if at all, are these assumptions themselves to be vindicated?

In *The Gay Science,* Nietzsche arraigns human beings for what he calls their "four errors"; that is, of always having seen themselves imperfectly; of attributing to themselves qualities

---

the "elect," the "reprobate," and the "redeemed"; I believe these are the exact equivalent of the three animals of Nietzsche's allegory.

2. R. J. Hollingdale, "Introduction" to F. Nietzsche, *Thus Spake Zarathustra* (Harmondsworth: Penguin Books, 1969), 13.

they do not really have; of setting themselves mistakenly "above" nature and the animals; and of constantly inventing new sets of values, each of which has been taken to be absolute, but in fact has amounted merely to the arbitrary overvaluation of some particular set of human drives. To root out the effects of these four errors, he declares, is to do away with "humanity, humaneness, and human dignity."[3] On the nihilist interpretation, the effect of Nietzsche's writing is to destroy "humaneness and human dignity" once and for all. From the perspective of the New Enlightenment, once one has corrected what is in fact erroneous in Nietzsche's "four errors," one will be in a position to envisage and work for the real dignity of human beings. (It is of course to be noted that in fact we regard—and in my opinion are right to regard—Nietzsche himself as a being of outstanding human dignity.)

As to the first "error," there is no doubt that to envisage oneself and humankind as they really are, rather than falling headlong into damaging misapprehensions about one or the other, requires considerable skill and application. And the difficulties in the way are made worse than they would otherwise be by the fact, pointed out notably by Socrates, that we are prone to pretend to knowledge about matters of which we are in fact ignorant. The primary means of avoiding such ignorance is to work out a reliable basis for forming true beliefs about ourselves. The assumption—apparently adopted from Nietzsche by that great Nietzschean Sigmund Freud—that we see ourselves rightly when we acknowledge that rationality and morality are illusions,[4] should be recognized for the calamitous,

3. *The Gay Science* (New York: Random House, 1974) 115; cf. Hollingdale, loc. cit.

4. This seems to be implicit in Freud's claim that the mind really consists of what he calls "the id," which actually determines the "higher" "ego"-processes of which we are conscious. Cf. Hugo Meynell, *Freud, Marx and Morals* (New York: Barnes and Noble, 1981), 106.

but fortunately self-destructive, error that it is. And the reason is simply this: denial that we believe anything that is true, or have good reason for any of our beliefs, is incompatible with itself; and we have as sound reasons for believing that some actions and states of affairs are better than others as for any of our other beliefs.

On the basis thus provided, we will be able progressively to determine what are the real, and what are the merely imaginary, human qualities, and so avoid the more egregious consequences of the second error listed by Nietzsche. It is of course to be noted that, in the very act of stigmatizing some of our supposed qualities as "imaginary," we tacitly presuppose that we are at least in principle able to determine which of these qualities are real. Otherwise the term "imaginary," which involves a contrast with what is real or genuine, would itself be bereft of significance. As for the third of the alleged "errors"—once we have determined what our real qualities are, we can go on to establish our actual place in the hierarchy of nature. If it is doubted that there is such a hierarchy, it should be noted that we do, for better or for worse, possess rationality and moral responsibility, in a manner in which rocks and trees, and even bats and cats, do not. In this respect, indeed, humanity is unique among the biological species in our part of the cosmos; rather than letting these special qualities atrophy or allowing them to pervert or strangle our instincts, we can aspire to a relatively happy and fulfilled life, both for ourselves and for others, by cultivating a harmony between reason and passion. (With regard to the last point, Nietzsche's own splendid teaching about sublimation is particularly germane, as we shall see.) We may also work toward a delightful and mutually enhancing relationship between ourselves and non-human animals, plants, and the rest of nature; mere domination of the non-human world is miserable as well as fatal in the long run. Of the two ideals of science, the will to understanding and the will to control, the second certainly has its place—we should not have to put up with variola, or endure unprotected the rigors of the Alberta winter—but for the spiritual good of humankind it is essential that it be subordinate to the first.[5]

The fourth supposed "error" is closely related to the most crucial ambiguity in Nietzsche's position. He appears sometimes to imply that all values, including the value of truth, are equally subjective and arbitrary. But at other times he seems to be exhorting us, in a manner quite inconsistent with the preceding, to adopt a new scheme of values which, unlike most of the old ones, encourages us to realize our best and noblest potentialities.[6] The second way, in my view, is the one which plainly ought to be followed, for all that the first is so fashionable in these postmodernist and deconstructionist times. And any tradition, however revered, that prevents the realization of the best human potentialities ought to be repudiated or at least substantially modified. As a Catholic priest remarked in my hearing a few years ago, human beings are quite right to rebel against any deity who binds Prometheus to his rock and sets the vultures on him. On the basis of the wealth of psychological knowledge that has been gained during the present century, we have to examine the various "tables of morality" to determine how far each promotes human happiness and autonomy consistently with fairness, and how far it militates against them. (Of course there are differences in the backgrounds and cultures of human groups, which have to be taken into account when we do this; but some traditional practices, in the light of what we now know about the factors affecting human happiness and

5. Martin Heidegger has many useful things to say on this matter; but in my view he identifies the scientific attitude as such too much with the ideal of domination and control. See Hugo Meynell, *Redirecting Philosophy* (Toronto: University of Toronto Press, 1995), chap. 9.

6. This ambiguity is nicely caught by a passage in *The Antichrist* (6, first half), where he at once excoriates human depravity as he conceives it and denies that he is making any moral judgment in doing so.

misery, are bad, and have to be contested by all means the implementation of which would not have consequences still worse than the evil to be remedied.)[7]

Nietzsche will have it that the desire for truth, in common with all other human propensities, is an expression of the will to power.[8] At one point Zarathustra subjects his remarkably docile audience to the following harangue: " 'Will to truth' you call it . . . ? A will to the thinkability of all being: this I call your will. All being you want to *make* thinkable: for you doubt, with well-founded suspicion, whether it is thinkable. Yet it shall yield and bend for you. . . . That is your entire will . . . a will to power—also when you speak of good and evil and valuations."[9] Of course, the moral is to be applied to philosophy—including, presumably, Nietzsche's own: "Philosophy is this tyrannic urge itself, the most spiritual will to power."[10] According to the New Enlightenment, as we shall see, there is excellent reason to suppose that "being" is intrinsically "thinkable," since it is nothing other than what true judgment is actually or potentially about, and what well-founded judgment tends to be about. As for the view that the search for truth is just one more expression of the will to power, either the search is completely disqualified due to this fact, or it is not. If it is, we could have no reason to believe that any statement that we made was true, even the

7. For example, however deeply it was established within a culture, and with however many incidental goods it was there associated (say, enabling a woman to find standing among her peers, or to marry and so find economic security), I take it that the old Chinese custom of foot-binding was bad. The reason is that it caused considerable pain, and greatly diminished the freedom of those subjected to it, without any commensurate good being brought about by means of it.

8. I may note in passing that I regard Nietzsche's attempt to reduce all drives to the "will to power" (cf. Kaufmann, *Nietzsche,* 198) as a confusing distraction from the more useful elements of his thought.

9. Nietzsche, *Zarathustra,* 113.

10. *Beyond Good and Evil,* 9; cited in Kaufmann, *Nietzsche,* 176.

statement that all truth-claims are disqualified by the fact that they are motivated by the will to power. If it is not, one needs some means of determining in what circumstances the will to power disqualifies truth-claims, and in what circumstances it does not. I shall argue in the next chapter that truth-claims are well-founded, and so liable to be true, so far as they are arrived at as a result of attention to relevant evidence, envisagement of a range of hypotheses, and judgment in each case as true of the hypothesis that is best corroborated by the evidence. If power is exerted, as it may be, to foster this process, it does not tend to vitiate truth-claims made in deference to it; so far as it is exerted to obstruct the process, it does. Walter Kaufmann's coy admission, that Nietzsche "never worked out an entirely satisfactory theory of knowledge,"[11] appears to me to be a considerable understatement.

Nietzsche sometimes suggests that human beings may actually be incapable of discovering truth, and he toys with the idea that our most fundamental categories may misrepresent reality in the interests of our comfort and convenience. As he puts it, "We have arranged for ourselves a world in which we are able to live—with the postulation of bodies, lines, surfaces, causes and effects, motion and rest, form and content: without these articles of faith nobody could now endure to live! But that does not mean they are something proved and demonstrated."[12] Now it must be admitted that, in a strict sense of "proof," nothing can be proved without appeal to premisses, which in turn cannot be proved without appeal to further premisses; and one cannot provide such premisses *ad infinitum.* Conversely, with the right premisses, one can prove any weird assertion whatever. Suppose that it is required to prove that all cows are Members of the British Parliament. Let us take as our premisses, that all cows

11. Kaufmann, *Nietzsche,* 177–78.
12. *The Gay Science,* 121; Hollingdale, 13–14.

are British ministers of the Crown; and that all British ministers of the Crown are Members of the British Parliament; it follows from this, as a matter of strict logic, that all cows are Members of the British Parliament.

However, we do *have good reason to believe* that there are bodies, surfaces, forms and contents, causes and effects, and so on, in the world. If ever there is a place in philosophy for arguments in the manner of G. E. Moore, this is surely one of them. Moore inferred from the doctrines of idealism that it was problematic whether he really had two hands. He showed his audience that he had two hands; and that, so far as he was concerned, was the end of the matter.[13] If there were no bodies, I would not have been holding a hard-boiled egg in my hand just before I wrote the first draft of this sentence. But I *was* holding a hard-boiled egg in my hand at that time. So there are bodies in the world. If there were no surfaces, then the egg would not have felt cool and brittle to my touch. But the egg did feel cool and brittle to my touch. Therefore there are surfaces. If there were no causal relations between events, I would not have been able to break the shell of the egg by knocking it against my desk. But I was thus able to break it; therefore there are causal relations between events, and so causes and effects. And so on, and so on. It is true that we are often apt to falsify reality, and to deny the splendor and terror of much of our experience (which I believe is actually Nietzsche's primary concern), by means of the conceptual apparatus that we set up. (The art-critic Roger Fry complained that people are apt just to read the labels on things, rather than to experience them for what they are; he rightly maintained that it was a main function of the arts as to counteract this tendency.)[14] But we cannot really even conceive

13. See G. E. Moore, "Proof of an External World," *Philosophical Papers* (London: Allen and Unwin, 1959), 146–50.

14. Roger Fry, *Vision and Design* (Harmondsworth: Penguin Books, 1960), 10, 25. Dickens has similar things to say about his craft as a novelist; cf. Hugo

of ourselves as doing so, without having some inkling at least of what it would be like to have a conceptual apparatus that hit off reality comparatively rightly, or was *not* a means of suppressing or denying experience. I believe that, underlying Nietzsche's view, there is the assumption that we would somehow come to confront reality directly if we opened ourselves to experience without using concepts at all. But I shall argue that this is a mistake; that reality is nothing other than what we tend, if we go about it in the right way, to apprehend in our judgments; and judgments can be framed only in terms of concepts.

It seems at first sight quite easy to conceive that the human conceptual apparatus might just as such radically misrepresent reality, or get in the way of experience. But if an "error" is not even in principle detectable, it is difficult to see how in the long run it could even count as an error. Error makes sense only as contrasted with a truth which at least conceivably might be available to us,[15] and such availability could only be by way of some conceptual apparatus or other. Nietzsche purports to embrace what he calls "ultimate scepticism," which leads him to ask, "What in the last resort are the truths of mankind? They are the *irrefutable* errors of mankind."[16] But there is a question whether what is in principle immune from refutation is really susceptible of being literally either true or false. And the idea of the will to truth as a kind of lust to impose our thought on reality depends on the assumption, which I will argue in the next chapter to be mistaken, that reality is somehow other than

---

A. Meynell, *The Nature of Aesthetic Value* (Albany: State University of New York Press, 1986), 58.

15. Nietzsche's false step at this point is of course closely related to the notorious Kantian error about "things in themselves" being unknowable to us. We cannot know that what is in principle unknowable to us is the cause of our experience, especially if the causal relation itself does not belong to things as they are, but is imposed by us on things, as Kant maintains, in the act of cognizing them.

16. *The Gay Science,* 265. Hollingdale, op. cit., 14.

what we tend to apprehend by our thoughts, so far as we subject them to thorough criticism in the light of experience. What applies to our inability to know what is true, of course, applies at least equally to our knowledge or implementation of any real "good."[17]

However, it would be wrong to maintain that Nietzsche was in general hostile to reason. Though he denied that reason is the basic drive—he assigned that function to the will to power—he did give it a special role with respect to the passions, as bringing order out of their chaos and promoting their harmonious integration. He commended reason as giving people power not only over other things and persons, but above all over themselves. Throughout his writings, he attributes dislike of reason to intellectual bad conscience. His hatred of philosophical systems is due to the irrationality which he finds in their proponents' failure to question their premisses. In fact he was inclined, as Kaufmann puts it, to "measure power and weakness in terms of man's willingness to subject even his most cherished beliefs to the rigours of rationality."[18] There is some question, of course, of how far this was consistent with some other attitudes and aims expressed in Nietzsche's writings.

But there is no doubt that, where moral matters are concerned, the main impression that one gets from Nietzsche is by no means arbitrary or nihilistic. He seems in fact to have been convinced that there is, latent in the nature of human beings, a real good which they ought to pursue, but which has been largely misrepresented by traditional moralities. Humanity as it is, Nietzsche's Zarathustra tells us, is something that is to be overcome; it would seem to the fully realized human being as

17. If one takes seriously the claim that "the controlling tendency of his thought was nihilist" (Hollingdale, op. cit., 13), the equal arbitrariness of all moral stances would seem to be the inevitable consequence.

18. Kaufmann, *Nietzsche,* 198–200.

funny as the ape does to human beings in the state that they now are. But he insists that the overcoming should not be, as it has so often been in the past, a matter of starving the bodily and the sensual; it should rather be one of realizing them and bringing them to perfection. Hopes of life after death for the ever-so-spiritual soul have been used (or abused) in this way, to corrupt and poison the potentialities of abundant embodied life here on earth. In fact it is weariness of life that makes people preoccupied with gods and afterlives. Despisers of the body are ultimately victims of disappointment; they are by no means witnesses or bridges to the superhuman. What we like to call our "reason" and our "goodness" are such as to stunt humanity; to limit us to the state in which we are now, rather than to realize what we have it within us to be. It is not what we think of as our "sin," but our meanness even as sinners, which is the real abomination. What we are pleased to think of as our virtues are largely means for the preservation of the quiet life.[19]

One thing that especially distracts us from self-realization, as Zarathustra sees it, is the so-called virtue of love of our neighbor. The fact is that love of our neighbor is apt to be a pretext for clinging to the worst and meanest side of ourselves, and the company of others may be a distraction from the solitude that would force us to take stock of how it really is with us.[20] The real friend, who brings out the best in us, fostering our originality and creativity rather than encouraging our laziness and cowardice, is far more worthy of our love. The mob of one's "neighbors" is always warning that to seek is the way to get lost, that to be solitary, unique, or original is the way to perdition. Solitude can indeed be hard; many will have to change their opinion

19. Nietzsche, *Zarathustra,* 12–14, 28–29, 31, 35.

20. One may compare Pascal on the fear of being alone and undistracted, and so confronted with oneself, and the fundamental misery of the human condition. Cf. Blaise Pascal, *Pensées* (Harmondsworth: Penguin Books, 1966), 67 (Fragment 136).

of the individual who strives to realize the best in herself, and will hate her for it. (One is reminded of the fact, well-known to psychotherapists, that those who are most stubbornly resistant to the patient's recovery are often the patient's family members.) And indeed, the higher you go, the smaller you will appear to the envious. But you yourself are your own worst enemy; the greatest obstacles to self-realization, as well as the only means to it, lie within ourselves.[21]

One of Nietzsche's main complaints against Christianity is that it has tried to cope with human desires by tearing them out at the root, rather than by finding out and fostering the best potentialities within them. On the dictum of Jesus, that a person should cut off a part of her body which offends her,[22] Nietzsche comments: "The logic is: the desires often bring great harm, thus it follows that they are evil and to be rejected. . . . And the same goes for the moralists' mania which demands not the control but the extirpation of the passions. Their conclusion is ever: only the emasculated man is the good man."[23] Kaufmann perceptively remarks that some of Nietzsche's more outrageous comments seem less so when regarded in the light of his detestation of emasculation as a human ideal. It is often stated and deplored that Nietzsche admired Cesare Borgia. But his point was, surely, that it is absurd as well as monstrous to consider Borgia as unhealthy and an emasculated man as healthy. When asked to clarify this point, Nietzsche said that he was not in favor of abolishing all decent moral feelings, but he did wonder whether our conviction that we were more morally virtuous than some notorious characters of the past was not really just a sign that we were more emasculated. Perhaps we are simply too weak to be evil.[24] As to how a proper control of the passions

21. Nietzsche, *Zarathustra,* 60, 61–62, 64.
22. Mark 9:43.
23. *The Will to Power,* 383; Kaufmann, *Nietzsche,* 193.
24. Kaufmann, *Nietzsche,* 193–4.

may be achieved, Nietzsche was the first to use the term "sublimation" in the sense popularized by Sigmund Freud and the psychoanalytic movement.[25] One should cultivate one's emotions and desires—rather than destroying them or letting them run to seed—like a gardener; and in fact, as Nietzsche says, we find people cultivating the gardens of their instincts and emotions with more or less taste.[26] He mentions a number of ways by which desires can be controlled, apart from self-mortification—avoiding opportunities for their indulgence, generating oversaturation and disgust, associating them with painful thoughts (like those of disgrace or humiliation), or diverting one's attention to another form of delight or to an exacting task.[27] The sexual impulse may be thus diverted into scientific or artistic creativity; the desire to defeat or torture one's foes into rivalry between athletes, playwrights, or philosophers.[28]

Nearly all the points I have culled from Nietzsche's work in the last two paragraphs are, of course, grist to the mill of the New Enlightenment. Whether this destructiveness of human life as lived on earth is of the essence of Christianity and of belief in an afterlife, or rather a deadly perversion of either or both, is a question of the utmost importance, which I do not wish to take up at present. Oddly enough, although Nietzsche identified himself fundamentally as an anti-Christian, Ludwig Klages's remarks, which he meant disparagingly, about "the Christian in Nietzsche," are not completely wide of the mark. Nietzsche is as insistent as the most ascetic of Christians on the need to "undergo," to endure solitude, suffering, and humiliation, if we are to come to our true selves, the fully realized persons that we have it in us to be. But Christianity as he con-

25. Ibid., 188.
26. Nietzsche, *Dawn,* 560; cf. Kaufmann, *Nietzsche,* 191
27. Ibid., 109; cf. Kaufmann, *Nietzsche,* 190.
28. Kaufmann, *Nietzsche,* loc. cit.

ceives it prevents rather than promotes the realization of this desirable end, destroying the best in human life rather than enhancing it.

To sum up the central thesis I have been trying to establish—that there are two divergent and ultimately incompatible tendencies in Nietzsche's thought—I shall invent two philosophers, called Naetzsche and Noetzsche, each holding a set of ideas consistent within itself, but by no means compatible with that set maintained by the other.[29] I believe that the question—Which represents the real Nietzsche?—is unanswerable and tends to distract the mind from more important matters.[30] Naetzsche proclaims that human beings have generally been thoroughly mistaken about what kinds of human character, and what dispositions to action, are good or bad, and in consequence about the way in which people ought to conduct their lives; this is due to cowardice, self-deception, a covert resentment of genuine human excellence, and other disreputable motives. Christianity is especially to blame, as preventing people from self-expression and self-realization by its demands for humility and self-abasement, and as condemning the life of the senses and passions by a punitive asceticism backed by false promises of recompense in an afterlife. The net result, to quote R. D. Laing, is an effective equation between goodness and inner deadness.[31] Not that heroic self-discipline is by any means discouraged by Naetzsche; but its aim should be to direct and harmonize our passions and desires, to "sublimate" them, not

29. This paragraph and the next largely repeat what I have written in "On Nietzsche, Postmodernism and the New Enlightenment," *New Blackfriars* (January 1995), 15–17.

30. Letitia Meynell makes the interesting suggestion that the sources for Noetzsche's position are to be found mainly in works of Nietzsche's middle period, such as *Beyond Good and Evil* and *The Gay Science.*

31. See R. D. Laing and A. Esterson, *The Families of Schizophrenics* (London: Tavistock Publications, 1964), 47, 52; Laing, *The Divided Self* (Harmondsworth: Penguin Books, 1965), 181, 183.

to destroy them. Genuine human virtue depends on a relentless honesty, which constantly criticizes what merely has the appearance of truth or goodness; such virtue heads for knowledge and implementation of what is really true and good. What Naetzsche ought to say, and would say if he were not hobbled by Noetzsche, is that what such truth and goodness are is not simply up to you or me or us; further, means can in principle be spelled out by which this criticism, which takes us from ignorance or self-deception to knowledge, may be accomplished. Systematic thought in science or philosophy, for all its liability to abuse, is a necessary condition for knowledge once knowledge has reached a certain level of sophistication; the abuses may be corrected by a constant willingness to test one's system in the light of experience. Naetzsche will be passionately irreligious or atheistic, so far as he thinks that there is no good reason to espouse religion or to believe in God, or that such belief is essentially destructive of human authenticity; but he might just conceivably be religious or theistic, if he thought otherwise.

According to Noetzsche, what is "true" and what is "good," and the methods by which they are to be known and implemented, are up to you or me or us to decide. No truth-claim, whether in the realm of fact or value, is anything more than an expression of the claimant's will-to-power or aesthetic preference. Alleged "truth," particularly when expressed within some system of concepts or ideas, is a matter of control—of imposing the reassuring stabilities of reason on the terrifying and invigorating flux of reality or experience, or of more or less tacitly subduing other people to one's will—rather than of reflecting what is actually so. What Noetzsche ought to say, and would say if it were not for the salutary corrective supplied by Naetzsche, is that, since the previous sentences of this paragraph are judgments which are themselves merely expressive of aesthetic preference or will to power, one might just as well state the contradictories if it takes one's fancy or appears to be an effective means to self-aggrandisement. And the same goes for every other judgment of fact or value: we might as properly opt for cowardice or self-mutilation as for courage and self-enhancement. Since no judgment whatever, whether factual or evaluative, can be made for good reason, and so its contradictory is just as well founded, one must end up, like Cratylus, making no statements at all. (What after all is the point of making any statement, if there is just as good reason for stating its contradictory? One can, of course, mouth phonemes, syllables, or even words; what are ruled out are ordinary indicative sentences, to the effect that something is or is not the case. Questions also appear impossible, so far as they are about *whether* something is the case; so do commands and requests, inasmuch as they are attempts to *get* someone else to *make* something to be the case. Even doubts seem to be put out of court, since they make sense, as Augustine noted, only as concerned with whether something is or is not the case.)[32] Since the real world, if there was one, would exist, and be largely as it is, prior to and independently of the worldviews that are expressive of the various wills to power of their purveyors, and our "knowledge" can attain to no such thing, we have no reason to suppose that there is any such "real world." Whether Noetzsche was religious or not would be a matter of arbitrary fancy.

I put it to the reader that if Naetzsche is an outstanding prophet of the New Enlightenment, Noetzsche is a main progenitor of postmodernism. I hope to amplify this suggestion throughout the rest of this book.

32. *Contra academicos,* in *Writings of St. Augustine,* vol. I, ed. and trans. L. Schopp (New York: Cima Publishing House, 1948), 154.

2

ELEMENTS OF THE NEW ENLIGHTENMENT

IT WOULD generally be agreed that our notions of what is true as opposed to false, and good as opposed to bad, are easily subject to error and need constant criticism. We may change our minds, for one reason or another, about whether it is true that Venus' average surface temperature is more than two hundred degrees higher than that of the Earth, or whether it is true that the accused has poisoned her husband, or that the leader of Her Majesty's Opposition has accepted a bribe in the last couple of weeks. We may also alter our opinion about whether capital and corporal punishment are ever right; whether active homosexuality is so wrong that it should not be socially condoned; or whether Marxist socialism is the best political option.

It is difficult to see how anyone could deny that some of these changes of opinion are more justified than others. A person who had previously taken the Book of Genesis as an accurate account of the origin of life on earth might visit a museum of palaeontology and be unable to persuade herself that the whole set-up was an elaborate fraud—and so conclude that something like the Darwinian theory of evolution was the more likely possibility.

Perhaps the evidence assiduously unearthed by a detective and presented to a court can hardly be explained otherwise than on the assumption that the victim's wife was not guilty, but was framed by his second-last mistress, whose infatuated present lover did the fell deed on her behalf. A careful survey of the relevant data may seem to be subversive of the hoary assumption that corporal punishment of youths for minor misdemeanors usually has a salutary long-term effect on their behavior. A consideration of societies claiming to be Marxist could suggest that the noble ideals of Karl Marx, or those attributed to him, are unworkable in practice and do not lead to the just and happy state of society that he anticipated. (The point is not, it should be noted, that all of these changes of opinion issue in true belief—only that people do change their opinions in the light of evidence, and that it is proper that they should do so.)

Can we point out norms according to which such criticism of our judgments of fact and value is to be carried out? At first sight, at least, it seems obvious that we can. On all these questions, various as they are, it is relevant to be *attentive* to sensation or feeling; to be *intelligent* in envisaging possible explanations; and to be *reasonable* in revising, rejecting, or reaffirming our opinions so far as they are or fail to be the explanation which best fits the evidence. The reader may easily confirm that this schema may be applied to all of the above instances of persons changing their opinions.[1] What I shall call "the New

1. In what follows, I shall use the term "New Enlightenment" for the implications of this view of the mental process that underlies changes of opinion of the sort that may result in knowledge. To distinguish it clearly from the New Enlightenment, the configuration of ideas usually referred to as "the Enlightenment" will be called the "Old Enlightenment." The term "New Enlightenment" is due to Professor Frederick Lawrence. A comprehensive and meticulously argued account of the New Enlightenment and its ramifications is to be had in *Insight. A Study of Human Understanding,* by Bernard Lonergan (Toronto: University of Toronto Press, 1992). For an overview of that great work, see Hugo Meynell, *An Introduction to the Philosophy of Bernard Lonergan*

Enlightenment" is a matter of articulating and justifying these norms, and applying them to the whole range of human beliefs and attitudes.

Now it is usual for the advocates of postmodernism to deny that there are such universal norms, and it is apparently characteristic of the "deconstruction" allied to it to subvert all those "binary oppositions" in which their use would appear inevitably to issue. The doctrine that we apply such norms, and can make ourselves aware that we do so, may be said to be vitiated by the "myth of presence," which, on Jacques Derrida's account, so radically compromises the pretensions of Western thought.[2] In what sense, if any, can these mental processes which I have listed and briefly described be said to be "present" to us? Well, we seem to be *aware of* them to some degree at least. It is obvious that I may be aware of such things as the touch of my shirt on my back; a slight feeling of numbness in my calf; the rhythmic clicking of the windshield wipers in the bus where I write the first draft of this sentence. But I am also aware of the puzzlement to which a course of sensations or feelings may give rise—why did that germ-culture in my laboratory catch mold, or why did I feel so annoyed for a moment when my wife reported a successful business deal she had carried through? I may also be aware of the "aha experience," as it has been called, when I

(Toronto: University of Toronto Press, 1992). (It should be noted that the term "New Enlightenment" does not occur in the writings of Lonergan himself.)

2. Inferring what Derrida *implies* presupposes a more or less determinate idea of what he *means*. But any such idea seems incompatible with his repeated insistence (or apparent insistence) on the indeterminacy of all interpretation. This is why my own accounts of his views will generally be accompanied by qualifications—"Some say that it is to be inferred from Derrida's position," "Derrida's apparent disapproval of what he calls 'the metaphysics of presence,' " and so on. Whatever Derrida *really means,* if indeed he "really means" anything, it can hardly be denied that his texts have been influential upon those who may usefully be labelled as "postmodernists."

envisage a possible explanation—perhaps the sample was not properly isolated; perhaps I am repressing jealousy of my wife's success. But evidently it is one thing to envisage possible explanations for some phenomenon; it is another to judge that one of these explanations is probably correct—I may confirm or falsify my hunches by examining the adequacy of the precautions used in my laboratory, or bringing to mind past instances of my immediate emotional reactions to the professional successes of my wife. Not only am I aware of all these kinds of mental activity, but I can make myself more so by suitably directed attention.[3] If Derrida or his disciples wish to deny that these mental contents and acts are "present" to me in the sense that I have given, they would appear to be wrong.

But it is just this sense of "presence" that is relevant to the problem of the nature and foundations of knowledge. How can we really know, it may be asked, what we all assume as a matter of course: that our knowledge is or can be of a real world that exists and that is as it is largely independently of ourselves and our mental processes? The answer is, briefly, that the real world is nothing other than what true judgments *are* about and well-founded judgments *tend to be* about; and judgments are well founded, and so tend to converge on truth, so far as they are arrived at attentively, intelligently, and reasonably in the senses that I have given.[4] We have excellent reasons for judging that there are many things in the universe—white-dwarf stars, magnesium, bee-eaters, and igneous rocks—that not only are other than ourselves, but do not depend for their existence and nature on our capacity to make well-founded and true judgments about them. We can similarly make well-founded and true judgments as to what persons, situations, or actions (Pope Alexander

3. Lonergan, *Insight,* XI, 1.

4. Ibid. For a contemporary objection to this view, see the "Note" at the end of this chapter.

VI, the hungry being fed and the naked clothed, imprisoning people for their religious faith or sexual orientation) are good or bad. And, as I have already said, the basic procedures by which we get to make such judgments are certainly in some sense present to our minds—at least sufficiently so, as I would maintain, to form the basis of knowledge.

A word seems in order here about the hoary philosophical problem of the possibility of our knowledge of an external world. Bertrand Russell wrote: "Empiricism and idealism alike are faced with a problem to which, so far, philosophy has found no satisfactory solution. This is the problem of knowing how we have knowledge of things other than ourself and the operations of our own mind."[5] The New Enlightenment solves the problem by distinguishing sharply between the experience or awareness we have of our own sense contents, feelings, and mental activities on the one hand, and the world knowable by reasonable judgment, of which we with all our thoughts and feelings form a very tiny and insignificant part, on the other. I can find excellent reason to judge that, if I were suddenly struck blind, the red and yellow mug that I see immediately to my right would go on existing and being red and yellow, and that other persons and physical objects will go on existing in much the way that I am used to after I am dead and therefore presumably no longer able to perceive them. Once one is clear about the fundamental nature of reality as the potential object of verified judgment, and experience as providing clues to it, from which it is to be known by the operations of intelligence and reasonableness, the supposed difficulty about our knowledge of the external world simply vanishes.

It is characteristic of postmodernism to rejoice in "destabilizing" opinions and beliefs. Now it is heartily to be agreed that

5. Bertrand Russell, *A History of Western Philosophy* (London: Allen and Unwin, 1946), 635.

all judgments of fact or value should be subjected to rigorous critical appraisal and that none of them should be taken for granted. But it must also be insisted that the result of such a process, while it will certainly be to subvert many such judgments, may well be to corroborate others. That Australia lies to the south of New Guinea, that common salt is a compound of sodium and chlorine, that Michel Foucault and Jacques Derrida are or were fluent French speakers, that binding the feet of a young woman to prevent their growth is a bad practice, are, presumably, judgments which, being true, tend to be more and more confirmed, the more intense the critical scrutiny that is directed upon them.

Certainly, it is usually difficult, if not impossible, at once to engage in such mental activities and to attend to and ask questions about them. But first-order attention, questioning, and so on can be remembered with sufficient vividness for such second-order attention, questioning, and so on to be possible. Perhaps things are "present" to memory only in a Pickwickian sense; but this seems to be sufficient for the purposes of getting the hang of what it is to inquire, to hypothesize, to come to know or to believe what is true for good reason. For example, an hour or a week after some exhausting mathematical, scientific, historical, or legal inquiry, a person might well inquire into her inquiry, of what nature it was, what provoked it, and how it was brought, or was not brought, to a successful conclusion.

There is often felt to be something obscure about exactly what Derrida means by "the metaphysics of presence," and what he finds objectionable in it. But at least Derrida's strictures are usually taken to impugn "Western rationality," along with its pretensions to yield knowledge of what is really the case about the world and ourselves. However, given that the arguments I have just sketched about the basis of knowledge are sound, either Derrida's arguments are not themselves sound, or they are irrelevant to the points presently at issue, of whether there are foundations of knowledge, and the nature of such foundations.

One thing that has tended to foster postmodernist attitudes, at least within the philosophical community, has been the apparent breakdown of the empirical and rational foundations that underlay, or at least seemed to underlie, the Old Enlightenment (as we will here call the intellectual awakening of the seventeenth and eighteenth centuries that is usually termed "the Enlightenment"). Jacques Monod invoked what he called a "principle of objectivity," according to which logic and experience alone are the source of genuine knowledge of the world.[6] But as anyone with the smallest acquaintance with contemporary analytic philosophy knows, there is no logically valid deductive inference between any set of statements whatever describing a course of experience and any set of statements whatever describing an external world. If "inductive logic" is invoked at this point, one can only comment that the "problem of induction"—of how one moves appropriately from individual instances to a generalization, or from items of experience to a scientific theory—appears as contentious now among philosophers as it ever was. The radical empiricism that was fashionable earlier in this century purported to eke out logic and experience with the so-called "verification principle." But it is now notorious that this principle self-destructs. It states, in effect (many formulations have been tried and found wanting), that every meaningful proposition is such that either its truth follows from the meanings of its terms, or it may be verified or falsified through sense-experience. "All hoopoes are birds" is obviously meaningful by the first criterion, as it would be self-contradictory to assert that one had just seen a hoopoe while denying that one had just seen a bird. Most statements of science and

6. J. Monod, *Chance and Necessity,* trans. Austryn Wainhouse. London: Collins, 1972.

common sense fall into the second category; it is obvious in principle what course of experience would tend to verify or falsify the statement that the mixing of hydrochloric acid and caustic soda will result in a solution of common salt in water, or that there are at present rats resident in the province of Alberta. Radical empiricists deal with mathematical statements by putting them in the former category: the truth of "seven plus five equals twelve" is to be inferred directly from the meanings of "seven," "plus," "five," "equals," and "twelve."

Why should the verification principle self-destruct? Because there is no conceivable course of experience by which one could verify or falsify the statement (which could hardly be true merely by virtue of the meanings of its terms) that all meaningful statements that are not true merely by virtue of the meanings of their terms are such that they can be verified or falsified by some course of experience. The verification principle, in fact, is nonsensical or meaningless according to the criterion supplied by itself. An alternative candidate, for providing either foundations or a substitute supposed to do just as well, is fallibilism. (The most renowned exponent of fallibilism, the late Sir Karl Popper, used falsifiability as a criterion of demarcation between science and metaphysics, without dismissing the latter as meaningless; but the principle can be generalized.)[7] At this rate, every proposition that is to be taken seriously as telling us what is the case about the world must be such that, while it *could* be falsified in the course of sense-experience, *in fact* it has survived efforts to falsify it. It would generally be agreed in effect that, when one envisages two possibilities *a* and *b*, and *b* has some highly unexpected consequences that are incompatible with *a*, but these turn out to be the case, this gives rather good reason for affirming *b*. (If water were a chemical element rather than a compound, you would

7. Cf. Karl R. Popper, *Objective Knowledge. An Evolutionary Approach* (Oxford: Clarendon Press, 1972), 12, 29–30, 85.

not expect to be able to turn it into two other substances by electrolysis. That you can do so gives you good reason to believe that it is not a chemical element.) When there is no conceivable evidence that would tend to falsify one of two rival hypotheses as compared with the other, there is surely good reason to suspect that there is no actual difference between them, that their apparent difference is no more than a matter of words.

But the criterion of falsifiability has its own problems. How would one falsify the principle of falsifiability itself?[8] One might say, if it is merely a criterion for science and not for meaning as such, the problem of self-reference disappears. But the question still remains, How is it to be justified? How is it to be shown to be any more than an arbitrary assumption or claim about how we get to know the things and events of the real world?

The foundations of value judgments seem to be in a still worse state of repair than those of judgments of fact, whether in the realm of science or in that of common sense. An obvious candidate for the foundations of value judgments is the human experience of pleasure and pain, happiness and misery, which might be supposed to be related to the goodness or badness of persons, situations, actions, and policies, rather as scientific judgments are related to sense experience.[9] But there are well-known arguments, perhaps taken less seriously at present than they were a couple of decades ago, which are supposed to invalidate such a claim. It has been usual in this connection to invoke the "fact-value dichotomy," deriving in the first instance from a passage in David Hume's *A Treatise of Human Nature.*[10] Hume suggests that one cannot validly infer any judgment containing

8. See Paul Feyerabend, "Consolations for the Specialist," in I. Lakatos and A. Musgrave (eds.), *Criticism and the Growth of Knowledge* (Cambridge: Cambridge University Press, 1970), 215–18.

9. For a classic exposition of this view, see J. S. Mill, *Utilitarianism* (London: J. M. Dent, 1964).

10. *Treatise of Human Nature,* III, i, 1.

evaluative notions such as "good" and "ought" from any set of judgments not containing such notions. An argument to much the same effect was propounded by G. E. Moore at the beginning of the present century.[11] Moore claimed that every attempt to define "good" fell foul of what he called "the naturalistic fallacy." In a manner reminiscent of the suggestion I made at the beginning of this paragraph, the "utilitarians," notably Jeremy Bentham and J. S. Mill, had claimed that an action (let us say) is good so far as it promotes the greater happiness of the greater number. But Moore claimed that it would follow from this that it is never the case that an action is good when it fails to do so; yet we are often inclined to say this, when, for example, "punishing" an innocent person to appease a raging mob is at issue. In this case, one surely might well say that it was wrong to "punish" her, even if doing so did promote the greater happiness of the greater number. The hardened utilitarian could claim, of course, that in fact it was right after all, even if it went against people's intuitions to say so. However, if the definition were correct, counters Moore, to claim that the "punishment" was not good or right, while admitting that it did tend to promote the greater happiness of the greater number, would not even make sense. And surely such a claim does make sense, even if it is in fact wrong. So the proposed definition of "good" must be rejected. And just the same applies to any other definition of "good" that might be offered—as what is in accordance with the will of God,[12] or what tends to promote the evolution of the human species toward greater intelligence, beauty, health, or whatever.

Moore concluded that "good" was, as he put it, a "simple intuitable non-natural property," to be apprehended directly in things, rather as one perceives that an object is yellow. The

11. *Principia Ethica* (Cambridge: Cambridge University Press, 1956).
12. This view has been quaintly labelled "theological naturalism."

radical empiricists of the next generation, of course, had no use for such properties, though they took it that Moore's argument, to the effect that goodness was not definable in terms of other properties, was sound. They concluded that to say that anything was good was not strictly speaking to attribute any property or set of properties to it at all, but rather either to evince a positive emotion about it, or to commit oneself or influence others to take up a positive practical attitude to it. Conversely, if (for example) I say that beating up elderly persons in the street is bad, I am expressing my feelings of disapproval toward such behavior, and adding my mite to the social pressures inhibiting myself and others from engaging in it. The same applies to judgments of aesthetic value, as when I deny that Anselm Hüttenbrenner is a great composer,[13] or maintain that Michelangelo's *Piéta* is a magnificent sculpture.

Arguments like those summarized in the last five paragraphs have made many analytical philosophers conclude that knowledge, whether of fact or of value, is without foundations.[14] At first sight it rather obviously follows from this that "anything goes"—that all judgments are in the final analysis arbitrary, or at least ultimately based on premises or assumptions that are arbitrary. Though some philosophers have sought to contest this inference, their protestations seem unconvincing. After all, to say there are no foundations for our judgments is to imply that there is no more foundation for the claim that there is usually snow in Alberta in January, or that it is wrong to torture

13. This unfortunate man wrote many compositions, but his main claim to the attention of posterity is that he seems to have mislaid most of the scherzo, and all of the finale, of Schubert's "Unfinished Symphony." See *Grove's Dictionary of Music and Musicians,* Fifth Edition, ed. Eric Blom (London: Macmillan, 1954), IV, 420.

14. Cf. M. E. Williams, *Groundless Belief* (Oxford: Oxford University Press, 1977). A New Enlightenment assessment of this brilliant and erudite little book might well harp on the curious paradox, that the author seems to make every effort to provide grounds for the belief that beliefs are groundless.

cats for fun, than for the contradictories of these claims. There is an "orderly march and natural progression of views," as J. H. Newman put it,[15] from the claim that there are no foundations for our knowledge, to dogmatism, scepticism, or relativism in factual or theoretical matters, and cynicism, selfishness, and opportunism in practical affairs. Why try to establish one's beliefs or practices on a critical foundation, when it is admitted that there is none to be had?

The claim or assumption that there are no objective or universal norms that underlie, or ought to underlie, our judgments about what is true or good is of the very essence of postmodernism. It should be obvious that this is profoundly destructive of civilization, which is fundamentally a matter of a disposition to criticize human beliefs and behavior in the light of what is really true and good. I shall show this in more detail in the following chapters. But the objection may properly be made that, if the so-called "foundations" of what is known as "knowledge" have really been shown to be unsound, it is of no use deploring the consequences of the fact; we had better just put up with them and act accordingly. However, I believe that the view that they have actually been shown to be unsound is a delusion, and a dangerous one at that. The setting out of the real foundations of our knowledge of what is true and good, the demonstration that they are such, and the drawing out of their consequences, is the essence of what I shall call the New Enlightenment.

How could the foundations of knowledge themselves be founded? If they are themselves unfounded, how can they be anything but arbitrary? I have already mentioned attentiveness to experience, intelligence in envisaging possibilities, and reasonableness in judgment as being the foundations of knowledge. I have now to justify the claim that they are so. Very

15. J. H. Newman, *An Essay on the Development of Christian Doctrine* (London: Longmans, Green and Co., 1890), 193–94.

briefly, *the contradictory of the claim that they are so is self-destructive,* in the following way. Suppose someone were to deny that these are the foundations of knowledge. Has she (or her authority) attended to the evidence bearing on the subject? Has she envisaged various possible explanations of that evidence? Does she make her denial on the ground that it constitutes the most satisfactory of such explanations? If she does, then her denial is justified by that very mental process whose relevance to the business of justification she is denying. But if she does not, there is no point in taking any notice of her denial, any more than to any other judgment made without justification. And for there to be good reason for making a judgment, is for it to be confirmable by attentiveness, intelligence, and reasonableness in the senses of these terms already given. Therefore, insofar as they are due to such a mental process, one cannot deny with good reason that judgments are well founded.[16]

Judgments made for good reason converge on truth. This is well illustrated by the typical detective story. Initially, the data provided for the reader may appear to support the judgment, let us say, that Dr. Exe administered the fatal dose of poison. But the alert reader will be on the lookout for clues that tend to tell against this hypothesis. By the end of the story, she should agree with the detective in seeing that all the evidence taken together, including that which seemed to incriminate Dr. Exe, in fact establishes the guilt of Professor Wye beyond reasonable doubt. Something similar happens in the history of science. A well-informed person who understands the oxygen theory of combustion will be able to account for the data (e.g., the fact that metals are shiny) that once appeared to support the phlogiston theory, together with others that are incompatible with it (such as, calxes weigh more than their metals). The same applies clearly to Newton's cosmology in relation to Ptolemy's, and

16. Cf. Lonergan, *Insight,* XI, 6.

Einstein's in relation to Newton's. It is by being attentive, intelligent, and reasonable—let us say, being rational for short—that we tend to reach the truth about things. For what is it, in the realm of common sense, history, or science, to realize that, whereas one had previously been in error, one is now at least a little closer to the truth? It is nothing other than for one to have attended to evidence that told against the earlier account, to have envisaged a fresh possibility, and to judge that that possibility is better corroborated by the evidence taken as a whole than the one previously held.

Now it is said to be a corollary of Derrida's thought that "the reality behind concepts cannot be reached, that the point of arrival at this reality will always be deferred by the creation of another concept." As Derrida sees it, the Western philosophical tradition, up to and including Michel Foucault, has been in error; this error "consists of the belief that there is something present behind the concept, and that whatever does lie behind the concept (or behind the sign, or the word) can be reached."[17] But on the principles of the New Enlightenment, while there is no *other* reality than what is to be grasped by our concepts so far as we exercise as much rationality as possible in forming and revising them, we *can* thus grasp such reality, and it is in an important sense other than our concepts. There were horses and phosphorus before there were people around to form the concepts of "horse" and "phosphorus," though we needed the concepts of "horse" and "phosphorus" to get to know that there were. So far as the "metaphysics of presence"—as apparently pilloried by Derrida—implied that there is some means of knowing the real world otherwise than through and in terms of our concepts, then Derrida was right to impugn it.

Let us say that one is "rational" insofar as one is attentive, intelligent, and reasonable in the senses described earlier. "The

17. Roy Boyne, *Foucault and Derrida* (London: Unwin Hyman, 1990), 68.

actual world" or "reality" is and can be nothing other than what true judgments are about, and well-founded or rational judgments tend to be about. Further, judgments can be framed only in terms of concepts that have been excogitated by creative intelligence. (Most of us take for granted, and thus overlook, the very elementary feat of creative intelligence required to move from the experience of individual horses to the formation of the concept "horse"; this is similar in essence to, though obviously less impressive in degree than, the intellectual feats of Kepler or Lavoisier.) That is why the notion that has been of concern to philosophers since Kant, of "things in themselves" that have nothing to do with anything we could conceivably come to know, is in the last analysis an incoherent one. It seems to amount to the unproblematically actual world of the naive realist, stripped not only of the sensory qualities that are in essential relation with our perceptions, but also of the intelligible or theoretical qualities that have been invented to explain these by scientists. But things when stripped of all such qualities, as Fichte and Hegel rightly pointed out against Kant, amount to nothing at all. It is important to note how idealism follows from criticism of Kant's notion of "things in themselves"; if things are ineluctably dependent on their being sensed or conceived by conscious subjects, then they cannot exist at all apart from such subjects. However, if the idealist rightly insists on the creative role of intelligence in our apprehension of what we conceive of as reality, she neglects the role of reasonableness in establishing that some of our intellectual constructions are corroborated by the evidence, and so are confirmed as true of the world, or at least as tending toward the truth about it. By the threefold mental process described, we come to know about a world that exists largely prior to and independently of humanity and its sensations and mental processes—indeed, within which we and all our works play a very small and insignificant part. The universe is certainly not dependent on our minds, but the subjective idealist has at least a glimpse of the truth (as we shall see in due course): that the nature and structure of our coming to know is a vital clue to the nature and structure of the universe, which is nothing other than what is to be known.[18]

It would be quite wrong to dismiss the verification principle or fallibilism as mere errors from which nothing useful is to be learned; when qualified in a suitable manner, in the light of the New Enlightenment account of how we acquire knowledge, they provide good rules of thumb for enquiries of a common-sense, scientific, or scholarly kind. There is nothing to be deplored in the rather informal version of the verification principle that Wittgenstein claimed that he originally proposed to the Vienna Circle, to the effect that, when one is looking for the meaning of a proposition, it is often useful to consider what course of experience would tend to verify or falsify it. And both principles are applications of a maxim that is of the essence of empirical science: hypotheses that cannot be tested in the light of experience have no claim to belong to such science. (This was the objection Popper launched against the "theories" of Karl Marx and Sigmund Freud[19] in particular, that they incurred no risk from the course of experience, but could be reconciled with any conceivable course of observable events.) Both principles in effect stress, to employ the New Enlightenment terminology, that one has to be attentive to experience in order to be reasonable in judgment; and the principle of falsifiability emphasizes that the fully reasonable person will be especially on the lookout for any evidence that tells against the hypothesis she happens to espouse. (Charles Darwin kept a special notebook to record evidence against his own theories.)

A word is in order about the place of deductive logic within rationality as I have described it. Deductive logic is useful for *facilitating* the application of intelligence and reasonableness to

18. Cf. Lonergan, *Insight,* XIX, 8. 19. Popper, *Knowledge,* 38n.

experience in discovering the truth about things, but it cannot by any means *replace* them. Not only are the operations of intelligence, in generalizing and hypothesizing, not reducible to deductive logic, as has been notorious since the time of David Hume,[20] but deductions from hypotheses have to be matched with possible observations or experimental results before they can be falsified or corroborated. What is called "inductive logic" is nothing but a very confusing label for those aspects of intelligence and reasonableness that cannot be reduced to deductive logic. One may indeed render trivially true Monod's thesis, as cited above, by simply labelling as "inductive logic" what I have called intelligence and reasonableness; but nothing but a very misleading oversimplification is gained by doing so.

According to radical empiricism as represented by the Logical Positivists, metaphysics, or the general theory of being or reality, is nonsense; on Popper's falsificationist account, metaphysical views may be provisionally useful in providing speculations that can be hardened by the scientist into testable hypotheses. The metaphysics of the New Enlightenment is neither of these things; it is simply the obverse of its epistemology. It is what follows, from the nature and structure of the process of getting to know, about the fundamental nature and structure of what is in principle to be known. Coming to know, as is made particularly clear by the mature sciences, is a matter of corroborating intelligible theories in the light of experience. The real world is nothing other than an intelligible sum of intelligible things, properties and events, to be grasped by the mind at the ideal term of the questioning of experience. (One form of question—"What" or "Why is this?"—is to be answered by intelligence; the other—"Is this so, does this exist?"—is to be answered by reasonableness in the New Enlightenment

20. Cf. *Enquiry Concerning Human Understanding,* Sec. IV, Part II, para. 33.

sense.)[21] Metaphysics is a matter of setting out how the world must be merely by virtue of the fact that it is knowable; science, of setting out how it is found to be in detail.

The correct metaphysics may conveniently be labelled "critical realism." The various incorrect forms of metaphysics all mistake a part of the business of coming to know for the whole, or at least for what is essential to it. Materialists are right to insist that there is a real world that exists prior to and independently of our minds, but they cannot account for minds and their understanding of the world. Experience is the most obvious feature of knowing; empiricists are right to stress its relevance, but they commit the blunder of mistaking "what is obvious in knowing" for "what knowing obviously is."[22] The idealist rightly insists on the creative role of intelligence in our apprehension of reality, but neglects the role of reasonableness in establishing that some of its creations are corroborated by the evidence, and so are true of the world, or at least tend toward the truth about it.

A characteristic component of the materialism that derives from the Old Enlightenment is reductionism, to the effect that reality is "nothing but" Democritus' atoms and the void, or quarks and leptons, or matter-energy, or whatever is supposed at any time to be the basic raw material from which the universe as we know it is built. (The late Gilbert Ryle used to speak in this connection of "nothing-buttery.") But in fact the universe is intelligible in various ways at various levels, of which the higher depend on the lower—chemical elements depending on nuclear particles, life on a particular collocation of chemical elements, human mental activity as we know it on a particular

21. These four types of question are distinguished, and then reduced to two, at the beginning of Book II of Aristotle's *Posterior Analytics* (II, 2, 89b 36ff).

22. Lonergan, *Insight,* XIV, 4.3.

variety of life, and so on. In other words, Aristotle was basically right in thinking that the world was a hierarchy of intelligible things, properties and relations distinct from appearance, but to be known by inquiry into appearance. (That reality as opposed to appearance is intelligible as opposed to perceivable—perhaps the most important discovery ever made in philosophy—was especially emphasized by Aristotle's master Plato, and is the main matter at issue in his doctrine of "forms.") One puzzling and distressing consequence of the metaphysical materialism so often inferred from science is that it seems to eliminate real minds and values. As we shall see, postmodernism is largely a reaction to this and other spiritually deadening consequences of the limited rationalism that was central to the Old Enlightenment. The "rationality" of the Old Enlightenment is the bugbear of postmodernism; from the point of view of the New Enlightenment, the trouble with the Old is that it was not quite rational enough. That minds in principle cannot be reduced to mere complicated arrangements of the physical substances and processes they get to know, provides the basis on which the natural and human sciences are to be distinguished from one another within the New Enlightenment scheme. In the human sciences, the objects as well as the subjects of inquiry are beings capable of more or less rationality, and this rationality is not ultimately just a matter of their behavior or the states of their brains.

One broad and slippery path to postmodernism is opened by W. V. O. Quine's thesis, perfectly correct in itself, that no course of experiences could in itself conclusively falsify a particular claim about the real world. Any course of observations whatever can be made compatible with a belief if one is prepared to make enough changes elsewhere in one's network of beliefs. From this Quine infers his "holism," the view that a network of beliefs as a whole depends on the relevant observations as a whole, rather than particular beliefs depending on particular sets of observations.[23] The whole vast corpus of observable phenomena on which modern astronomy depends could at a pinch be explained in terms of the geocentric theory, if anyone could be bothered to work out the details of the explanation; the process by which paranoids can explain all apparently recalcitrant phenomena in terms of their delusions is closely analogous. ("The Ruritanian minority has a stranglehold on our national economy." "But, my dear Theodore, there is no evidence whatever for this." "That just shows how complete the stranglehold is.") Since it seems difficult at this rate to see how any set of observations could ever provide adequate reason for abandoning any theory about the world, this view easily leads to the thoroughly postmodernist position of Richard Rorty, who would deny that our scientific theories, whether individually or as a body, are or could be testable by appeal to observations that are in principle independent of them.[24]

The way through this impasse is to admit Quine's point about particular claims always being preservable at a pinch in the face of recalcitrant evidence, while denying his holism. This may be done as follows. Particular claims are related to particular sets of possible observations, in the sense that *the less* often the members of those sets turn out to occur, *the less* it is appropriate to retain the claim in question, *unless* there is especially strong observational evidence to corroborate claims elsewhere in the system of which the claim forms a part. The fact is that, with most accepted scientific theories, it is not really difficult to point out what observations tend to corroborate them and discredit their rivals. (How is one to account for the fossil record, short of singularly complicated and implausible assump-

23. Cf. Alex Orenstein, *Willard Van Orman Quine* (Boston: Twayne Publications, 1977), 18–19.

24. Cf. Richard Rorty, *Philosophy and the Mirror of Nature* (Princeton: Princeton University Press, 1979).

tions, if the world came into existence less than twenty thousand years ago?) Occasionally ambiguities arise for a while, as when one set of data strongly suggests the truth of one hypothesis, while another set seems to support another which contradicts the first. The red shift of the light from quasars appears to prove that they are among the most distant objects in the universe, but the intensity of the radio signals reaching us from them is a hint that they are not.[25] For a while, again, phlogiston theorists could point out some data that were better explained by their own views than by the rival oxygen theory, which later became universally accepted. But such anomalies seem generally at least to come out in the wash as science advances, just as they do in the circumstances of ordinary life.

The apparent incompatibility of ethical with scientific objectivity, which has haunted many thinkers influenced by the Old Enlightenment,[26] is easily resolved in terms of the New. I may find evidence that an action, policy, or state of affairs is good or bad, much as I may find evidence that there are traces of lead in my town's water supply. Good actions and policies tend to foster happiness and fulfilment, and to diminish suffering and frustration; that good cannot be precisely defined in terms of any proposed criterion taken *singly* by no means implies that its status as *one* such a criterion is illusory. As I have said, that an action or policy tends to promote happiness is excellent reason for supposing that it is good; that there are occasionally countervailing reasons, as in the case of "punishment" mentioned earlier (where what adds to the general sum of happiness may well be deemed to be wrong or bad because it is unfair) does not affect the issue. As John Wisdom used to say in his lectures, a

25. See Nigel Calder, *Violent Universe* (London: Futura Publications, 1975), 79.

26. For a recent example, see Bernard Williams, *Ethics and the Limits of Philosophy* (Cambridge: Harvard University Press, 1985).

thing may be a matter of other things without being exactly definable in terms of them. Corporal punishment of the young, which used to be almost universally approved of in educational circles, is now widely regarded as bad, on the specific grounds that it is now thought that the beneficial effects on the victim's behavior are outweighed by the long-term bad effects on that same victim. In fact, one can be as attentive, intelligent, and reasonable with regard to matters of value as to matters of fact, and so just as "objective." "Genuine objectivity," in judgments both of fact and value, "is the fruit of authentic subjectivity."[27] But it is in the context of ethics that a fourth basic kind of mental operation, *decision*—which may be more or less *responsible* (as understanding may be more or less intelligent, judgment more or less reasonable)—is of special significance. In responsible decision one sets oneself to act according to the value judgment at which one has rationally arrived. One may say that a human being is authentic so far as she is attentive to experience, intelligent in envisaging possibilities, reasonable in judging, and responsible in deciding. According to C. S. Peirce, logic is a part of ethics; what he meant by this is that to reason as well as you are able is one aspect of being morally good.[28] To put it in our own terms, one has to make a responsible decision in order to be thoroughly attentive, intelligent, and reasonable—one thinks of the intrepid criminal investigator or journalist who persists in her inquiries in spite of threats and reprisals, the politician who tells her electorate unpleasant truths they do not want to hear, or the scientist employed by a tobacco company who arrives at conclusions that do not fit her employers' self-

27. Bernard Lonergan, *Method in Theology* (London: Darton, Longman and Todd 1971), 292.

28. *The Collected Papers of Charles Sanders Peirce,* vol. VIII, ed. Arthur Banks (Cambridge: Harvard University Press, 1958), 255. See Vincent G. Potter, *Charles S. Peirce on Norms and Ideals* (Worcester: University of Massachusetts Press, 1967), 4.

image or commercial interest. Plato and Aristotle were right in seeing ethics and politics as closely allied to one another: the former being concerned with rationality and responsibility in relation to the private, the latter in relation to the public good. Unfortunately, it is notorious that individual or group interest may restrict rationality and responsibility in either or both spheres.[29]

Postmodernism may usefully be looked at as a set of related beliefs and attitudes that oppose the "modernism" that derives from the Old Enlightenment. Basically, a restricted and debilitating view of the norms of rationality has provoked a reaction in which such norms are (at least explicitly) rejected altogether. (Fortunately, none of the four authors whom we will take as representative of postmodernism is quite consistent about this, as we shall see.) In order to get what is at issue in perspective, it will be convenient to attend to another corollary of the philosophy of the New Enlightenment. This distinguishes between "'positions,'"[30] which are compatible in the last analysis with their own rational and responsible assertion, and "counterpositions," which are not thus compatible.[31] The sort of "scientism" that purports to use science to show that the mental life is an illusion, or a mere "epiphenomenon" of states of the brain, is one example of a counterposition, since science, as has already been pointed out, ineluctably depends on the very mental life it is alleged to expose as illusory. What applies to mind applies to values as well (since science depends not only on the use of minds, but on minds being used well), and it is difficult to see how science can get anywhere unless truth is accepted as a real

29. Lonergan, *Insight,* VI, VII, XVIII.

30. It will be convenient to keep this last word in quotes when it is used as a term of art in the critique of rival views by the philosophy of the New Enlightenment. When I use the word without quotation marks, it should be taken in the ordinary sense, where no value judgment is intended.

31. *Insight,* XIV, 1; XVI, 2; etc.

value.[32] Another good example is psychological behaviorism as represented by the work of the late B. F. Skinner, which implies that no one says or writes anything because it is rational and responsible for them to do so, but only because of a history of positive reinforcements acting on a set of inherited predispositions. But if this is the case, the moral must be applied to Skinner's work itself, and this would destroy the possibility of anyone really believing it for good reason.[33] In general, the Old Enlightenment had less than comprehensively critical assumptions about the grounds of reasonable judgment in matters of fact and value, the unfortunate consequences of which have driven postmodernists into denying that such grounds are really available at all. This is rather odd, as postmodernists cannot themselves avoid making judgments, either in the ordinary affairs of their lives or in their scholarly works; in fact it is typical of them to make rather severe moral judgments, often evincing what amounts to moral outrage, against what is sometimes called "Western rationality."

One typical aim of postmodernism, as of the "deconstruction" that is closely allied to it,[34] is so far as possible to "destabilize" meaning. The "position" in this matter is that all our opin-

32. The point has been made eloquently by Hilary Putnam; cf. *Realism with a Human Face* (Cambridge: Harvard University Press, 1991), 138, 141; *Renewing Philosophy* (Cambridge: Harvard University Press, 1992), 55.

33. This does not imply that there are no important positive lessons to be learned from Skinner's work; cf. Hugo Meynell, "Lonergan's Cognitional Theory and Method in Psychology," *Theory in Psychology* IV, 2 (1994), 105–23.

34. Christopher Norris has tried to drive a wedge between Derridean deconstruction and postmodernism ("Deconstruction, Postmodernism and Philosophy: Habermas on Derrida," in David Wood, ed., *Derrida: A Critical Reader* [Oxford: Blackwell, 1992]). Here he takes issue with "the widely-held view that deconstruction is a matter of collapsing all genre-distinctions, especially those between philosophy and literature, reason and rhetoric, language in its constative and performative aspects" (167). I will discuss this matter later on.

ions should be subject to stringent criticism in the light of evidence. But some of our judgments will be corroborated by this criticism as such that their contradictories are self-destructive in the manner described above; while some will be confirmed as the best available interpretation of all the relevant empirical evidence. The opinion that there was at least one giant planet outside the orbit of Saturn, and that vaccination was an effective weapon against the scourge of smallpox, did not prove to be erroneous when subsequently examined. The counterposition is denial that genuine criticism stabilizes some meanings and judgments. (What about the judgment, "criticism destabilizes all judgments"?) The paradoxical effect of judging, while alleging in effect that one is refraining from judging, is masked by the jokey, allusive, and self-ironizing style of many postmodernist authors, which makes it seem vulgar or tactless to select any judgment and ask how it is to be justified as any more likely to be true than its contradictory. This makes many of them (like Derrida and Lyotard) excel in some types of criticism of literature and the arts, where it is more useful to be allusive and suggestive than to establish conclusions. Such writings at their best foster attentiveness and intelligence; but it is characteristic of postmodernists in general to be neglectful of reasonableness, with its inevitable assumption that there is a real truth to be known and a real good to be sought after.

I shall emphasize throughout this book what most of us assume as a matter of course—our capacity to know what is so, and not merely so-for-us-and-other-members-of-our-culture; and to know and do what is good—and not just approved by ourselves or the most prestigious members of our society. I shall call these capacities, in accordance with New Enlightenment usage, "cognitive self-transcendence" and "moral self-transcendence."[35] The Old Enlightenment presupposes the possibility

35. See Lonergan, *Method,* 38, 45, 104, 114, 121–22, 233, etc.

of both forms of self-transcendence, but fails adequately to justify it; postmodernism in effect denies it; while the New Enlightenment states it, justifies it, and spells out its consequences. The notion of a world-for-us is in fact parasitic on the notion of the world *tout court,* and makes no sense except in contrast with it. The difference amounts to one between those things and events believed to exist or occur on the basis of a rationality taken just so far, and those things and events that would be supposed to exist and occur if rationality were pursued to an indefinite extent. The sparrow you see out of the window of your bus on the way to work is not just a sparrow-for-you or for-your-society; it is a being that exists in its own right, having its own role to play in an ecological system in which I and my reader play scarcely more significant roles; it is the venerable descendant of creatures like archaeopterix, the dinosaurs, and the first microorganisms that inhabited the Pre-Cambrian oceans. You are cognitively self-transcendent in that, in spite of your embeddedness in your cultural, social, and economic milieu, you can in principle get to know about it as it actually is. Omega-particles and pulsars were not in the "world-for-us" of anyone before the present century; but presumably they are in the real world (it is perhaps conceivable that another scientific revolution might find it rational to dispense with either or both of them), and if so, they have been in the real world for billions of years. As to moral self-transcendence, I may judge that is a bad thing to forbid women to enter professions for which they are qualified and temperamentally suited, and make my judgment on the grounds that it frustrates them themselves and deprives others of the benefit of their talents; this indicates that it is really and objectively bad, and not just bad-for-me or bad-for-our-group.

Richard Rorty is credited in this connection with the remark that we cannot get outside our own skins. But, in the relevant sense, this is just what we *can* do. To deny that we can do so seems merely to confuse the direct object of experience, on the one hand, with the object of the actual or potential judgment that we may make on the basis of our experience, on the other. By virtue of visual, tactile, and aural experiences, which are within our skins, we can make judgments about things that are mainly outside them. Where judgment is concerned, it is a nice question how far being within one's own skin makes an event more available to us; it is in fact much easier for most of us to make informed judgments abut the weather than about the state of our own kidneys.[36]

According to Jean-François Lyotard, what is central to postmodernism is suspicion of what he calls "metanarratives," or general schemes of justification such as Freudianism and Marxism. In accordance with the principles of the New Enlightenment, one should seek to develop "positions" and to reverse counterpositions[37] in all such metanarratives; this is to say, examine them on a comprehensively critical basis to see how far they represent the truth and are useful in bringing about the good. Now it is true and important that our present economic and social position, as well as our experiences and relations with caregivers when we were small children, can either encourage or put heavy constraints upon our rational and responsible autonomy. As I have argued elsewhere, the "soft" versions of Freudianism and Marxism, which point to this fact and draw out its implications, have a permanent and fundamental contribution to make to an understanding and improvement of human living in New Enlightenment terms. But "hard" versions,

36. People sometimes appeal to anthropology in support of the view that "the real world" is merely a self-serving euphemism for "the world as conceived by our society." But, of course, the very possibility of anthropology presupposes that there is a real world which exists prior to and independently of the beliefs and assumptions of our society about it, part of which consists of *other* societies with *their* characteristic beliefs and assumptions.

37. Cf. *Insight,* XIV, 1.

which claim or imply that what we may like to call "rational and responsible autonomy" is a mere mask of underlying socio-economic or biological processes, are self-destructive "counter-positions" in the New Enlightenment sense.[38] (Relevant to this point are the discussions in Freud's and Marx's writings of the relation between "primary" and "secondary" psychic processes on the one hand, and the economic and social "basis" to the "superstructure" of morality, law, religion, and so on, on the other.)[39] This may be shown very simply. One may consider the claim, "human 'rational and responsible autonomy' is in the last analysis simply a veneer over instinctual process." Is this claim advanced, and proposed for belief, on the ground that it is the most intelligent and reasonable assessment of the relevant evidence? If not, it is not to be taken seriously. But if it is, it presupposes the very thing that it denies: that at least some human beings have sufficient rational and responsible autonomy to acquire and maintain beliefs because there is good reason for them to do so.[40]

There is a question that has dogged the Old Enlightenment, but has never satisfactorily been resolved by it. How can an

38. Hugo Meynell, *Freud, Marx and Morals* (New York: Barnes and Noble 1981), chaps. 4 and 5; especially pp. 12–13, 101–3, 108–9, 115.

39. Louis Althusser may be said to have made his own the counter-position in Marx, Jacques Lacan that in Freud. Compare Christopher Norris's remark on Lacan's "insistence that language is *always and everywhere* marked by the symptoms of unconscious desire, so that any attempt to escape or transcend this condition is deluded at best, and at worst a technique of manipulative reason in the service of a harsh and repressive social order" (Norris, "Deconstruction," 169). The italics are in the original; but had they not been so, I would have added them.

40. In "Bulverism, or, the Foundation of Twentieth-century Thought," C. S. Lewis describes the great moment of insight in the life of one Ezekiel Bulver. At the age of five, "he heard his mother say to his father—who had been maintaining that two sides of a triangle were together greater than the third—'Oh you say that because you are a man.' " C. S. Lewis, *Undeceptions* (London: Geoffrey Bles, 1971), 225.

explanation of human behavior that treats human beings as merely elaborately organized parcels of matter be reconciled with the explanation of that behavior as due, at least to some extent, to rational and responsible agency? The "solution" proposed by the materialists of the French Enlightenment, and assumed as a matter of course by many contemporary scientists and some philosophers (how could one doubt what is so obviously true?), is that the latter kind of explanation is primitive and soon to disappear; alternatively, it will retain a place merely as a shorthand, useful for the ordinary purposes of living (rather as we still talk of the sun rising in post-Copernican times), for the real scientific explanation. But this is to be rejected as a counterposition, for the reasons summarized in the last paragraph.[41] The mind-matter dualism of René Descartes issues inevitably in the impossibility of interaction between the human being *qua* rational and responsible agent and *qua* physical organism. Descartes' "Occasionalist" successors inferred that the Creator had providentially set things up in such a way that whenever an agent freely intended to do anything (say, when I decide to stop writing this sentence and get some tea), the physical laws governing her body would be predetermined, owing to the laws and initial conditions instilled into the universe at its creation, to oblige. For all the palpable absurdity of this account, at least it has the merit of taking the measure of the problem. As Immanuel Kant saw it, physical determinism rules in nature; but "nature" is merely a matter of appearances, which result from the imposition of the categories of our understanding upon the raw material of sensation. So although as parts of

41. See B. F. Skinner, *Science and Human Behavior* (New York: Free Press, 1953); Paul M. Churchland, *Matter and Consciousness* (Cambridge: MIT Press, 1984). For a useful account of contemporary reductive philosophies of mind, see W. Lyons, "Modern Work on Intentionality," in J. J. MacIntosh and H. A. Meynell, eds., *Faith, Scepticism, and Personal Identity* (Calgary: University of Calgary Press, 1994).

nature we are completely determined, in ourselves we may be rational and responsible. Indeed, we ought to believe that we are so in order that we may lead morally virtuous lives.[42] Kant's solution, of course, depends on a radical difference between things as they are in themselves on the one hand and things as we can in principle get to know them on the other[43]—a doctrine of his philosophy that, as well as being at a deep level incoherent (How does Kant on his own account know so much about what is unknowable?), has commended itself to very few of his successors.

In terms of the New Enlightenment, the problem is to be resolved in the following way. I mentioned earlier the New Enlightenment conception of the relation between the natural and the human sciences. In the former, the subject but not the object of inquiry is to be understood as to some extent rational and responsible; in the latter, both subject and object are so. It also acknowledges a real element of indeterminacy in physical process, which is such as to leave genuine options for human agents—in the sense that it may really be up to them whether or not to take a bribe, tell a lie, forgive a spouse, or protest against an act of cowardice or cruelty.[44] (The universe is apparently set up on the basis not only of "classical" laws—which determine exactly what will happen so long as certain conditions are fulfilled and nothing interferes—but also of "statistical" laws, which are a matter of the frequency of events of certain kinds: the emission of an alpha particle by a kind of radioactive atom, the incidence of psychosis among university professors.

42. I. Kant, *Critique of Pure Reason,* Preface to the Second Edition, B xxix.

43. Ibid., B xx.

44. The New Enlightenment would seem to issue in some kind of interactionism when it comes to the relations between the self as rational and responsible agent and the self as physical organism. Its view approximates to that expounded by K. Popper and D. Eccles in *The Self and Its Brain* (Berlin: Springer, 1977).

The determinism that haunts the Old Enlightenment is due above all to failure to infer the right consequences from the existence of statistical laws within our universe.)[45]

We are told that "the problem of reflexivity" is of the essence of "the postmodern predicament."[46] How can we reconcile our capacity to know and explain things with our liability to be explained as things? How can the scientist be the object as well as the subject of her own science? It is a central paradox arising out of the Old Enlightenment, that apparently we need to be cognitively self-transcendent to know and explain; but we are necessarily to be known and explained as cognitively non-self-transcendent, as, physically or socially, totally limited and determined. This dilemma has been left by the scientific movement of the Old Enlightenment as a kind of epistemological time bomb, which has finally exploded in the postmodernist resentment against rationality as impugning human freedom and self-determination. The New Enlightenment resolves the problem by pointing out that there is simply no difference between the subject as explainer—and more or less rational and responsible as such, and so cognitively and morally self-transcendent—and the subject to be explained, if one does not have erroneous beliefs or assumptions about the nature of knowledge. I can come to know about myself very much as I can come to know about the rest of the world—by intelligently conceiving and reasonably affirming what best accounts for the relevant data. That the data, including the mental acts I am aware of as applying to the data of sense or feeling, are sufficiently "present" for the purpose of knowledge, whether of myself or what is other than myself, I have already argued. The social milieu in which each of us exists imposes a set of concepts and judgments upon

45. Cf. Lonergan, *Insight,* II, 4 and 5.

46. Cf. Hilary Lawson, *Reflexivity: The Postmodern Predicament* (London: Hutchinson, 1985).

us, learned in the very process of acquiring our mother tongue, which is constituted by a mixture of rationality and responsibility with irrationality and irresponsibility. To that extent the social milieu puts us partly in the way of knowing, and partly in the way of failing to know, the truth about the world as it really is, and of knowing and failing to know, and doing and failing to do, what is good. Each individual can exercise her rational and moral autonomy, and so do her bit for social progress; or, she can fail to exercise it and thus contribute to decline.

It has often been pointed out, by friends and foes alike, that postmodernists have much in common with the "Sophists" who travelled about Greece in the time of Socrates and Plato. At that time and place, in a way that is very like how it is with us now in the West, there was a feeling abroad that the old values were being eroded, with moral and political chaos as the likely result. The fears of old-fashioned and conventional people were confirmed by the tendency of the Sophists to relativize all conceptions of what was true and good and to encourage in their students the cynical pursuit of personal gain, facilitated by the oratorical skills the Sophists had taught them. The view of Socrates and Plato, and of Aristotle after them, was of course quite different from this; by rigorous investigation, one could put both morality and factual knowledge on a firm foundation. But conventional persons, then as now, could easily identify their ruthless questioning of conventional beliefs and attitudes with the program of the Sophists.

Plato and Aristotle are in fact prophets, or rather perhaps representatives, of the New Enlightenment. One might say that the Old Enlightenment pursued their program, of a comprehensive knowledge and understanding of the world and of human affairs, in a thoroughgoing but lopsided way, upsetting the balance of matter, mind, and value in their philosophies, so that ultimately the science of matter was pursued in such a way as apparently to leave no room for either mind or value.[47]

In order to bring out the relation of Plato's philosophy to the New Enlightenment, it will be convenient to distinguish three aspects of his thought. The first of these has been clearly and compactly set out by Nicholas White: "The fundamental fact about Plato's theory of knowledge, from the beginning of his career to the end, is his conviction that there are matters of fact in the world, in some sense independent of our ideas and judgments, about which these ideas and judgments may be correct or incorrect. Plato's effort throughout his career was to expound this conviction, to explain what it seemed to him to mean and entail, and to defend it."[48] Let us call this view Platonism A; we may then say that it is very characteristic of postmodernists to be opposed to Platonism A, since they tend to deny any secure basis for knowledge, and apparently too an unequivocal body of facts in the world by virtue of conformity to which judgments are true and so constitutive of knowledge, by virtue of non-conformity to which they are false.

I shall mean by Platonism B all those additional doctrines attributable to Plato which are more or less confirmed by the New Enlightenment, including those which seem to be implicit in modern science. Chief among these are the propositions that reality as opposed to appearance is intelligible as opposed to sensible; that the real intelligibles (Plato's "forms") of which the world consists are to be known by inquiry into sensible appearances; that the mind must have sufficient independence of the material process with which it is so closely associated as to be able to apprehend these intelligibles; that mathematics is

47. Cf. Hugo Meynell, *Redirecting Philosophy* (Toronto: University of Toronto Press, 1998), chaps. 12 and 13.

48. Nicholas B. White, *Plato on Knowledge and Reality* (Indianapolis: Hackett Publishing Co., 1976), xiii. I owe this quotation to Onkar Ghate.

at least an important aspect of the language by which minds may grasp the intelligible; that reality partakes of universal essences rather than being merely a congeries of particulars; and that differences in value are differences in reality as opposed to mere appearance.

Platonism C consists of other doctrines associated with Plato,[49] like the undesirability of democracy, the ideal of the "philosopher-king," the necessity of censorship in a properly ordered state, a strict class system based on merit and natural aptitude, the need for a "midnight council" to detect and root out persons with the wrong opinions, and so on. What Plato says on subjects like this is always worth attending to, and perhaps especially when one vehemently disagrees with it. But the point I wish to make here is that these doctrines and attitudes are not at all obviously to be inferred from Platonism A or B. People often think of Plato and Aristotle as radically contrasted in their views, but evidently Aristotle would have strongly agreed with Platonism A, and, given a few important qualifications, with Platonism B. Perhaps it was not wholly unreasonable of Aristotle to maintain that he, and not Speusippus, would have been the proper choice as head of the Academy in succession to Plato.

Someone might object that the New Enlightenment is committed to a starry-eyed adulation of science, indulgence in which begs the question against postmodernism. I answer that, on the principles of the New Enlightenment, one is able to distinguish sharply between the maxims of comprehensive rationality, which give rise to science on the one hand, and on the other the reductionist materialism or "scientism" which is one of the worst intellectual monsters spawned by the Old Enlightenment. Such "scientism," so far from being, as is so often

49. In attributing opinions to Plato on the basis of his works, one should of course be cautious, due to the fact that he used the dialogue form.

supposed, a necessary consequence of the comprehensive application of rationality, is not even compatible with it. The New Enlightenment affirms the indispensable reality of attentiveness, intelligence, reasonableness, and responsibility, whereas a consistent scientism would deny their reality in the last analysis. The comprehensive rationality that is the essence of science at its best is worthy of starry-eyed praise; but scientism is to be repudiated in the strongest possible terms.

A related suggestion might be made, that what I have called "the New Enlightenment" is just one "form of life" among others, which cannot be argued to be superior to any other without begging the question. This suggestion I reject, for the following reason. There is no "form of life" which cannot be criticized in terms of basic principles, spelled out by the New Enlightenment, which determine how one is to arrive at knowledge of what is the case, and knowledge and implementation of what is good. The "form of life" practiced by the Aztecs involved tearing out the hearts of living human victims, on the understanding that, if this practice were to be discontinued, the courses of the heavenly bodies would change with catastrophic consequences on earth. Such a "form of life" involved infliction of intense suffering for no useful purpose; the conquistadores stopped the practice, but the expected catastrophe never materialized. The Nazi "form of life" also led to injustice and enormous suffering based on a false assumption, in this instance about the intellectual and moral character of human beings of different races.

It is to be concluded that "forms of life," and the "language games" characteristic of them, are based on assumptions about what is the case and what is worthwhile. The main issue between the New Enlightenment and postmodernism is whether or not there are general norms of rationality and evaluation by means of which one can test such assumptions and establish how well- or ill-founded they are. To argue the point in the New Enlightenment interest: either the grounds on which beliefs and attitudes can be evaluated—as probably or certainly true or false, good or bad—can in principle be expounded or they cannot. If they cannot, how can such evaluation be anything but arbitrary in the last analysis? The New Enlightenment spells out such grounds clearly and distinctly. But it is typical of postmodernist authors to oscillate between repudiating them on the one hand and taking them for granted on the other, as is illustrated a number of times in my detailed discussions of them. That evil and error are such potent forces in the world shows that we can afford to do neither.

The taking for granted by postmodernists of universal principles, of the kind that are spelled out and comprehensively justified by the principles of the New Enlightenment, is well illustrated by Lyotard's attitude to the Holocaust.[50] That Auschwitz was a bad business, one might say, is so obvious that the reasons why it was so do not have to be made explicit. But it is of some importance that they can in principle be spelled out; after all, the atrocities in question did happen, because persons did not believe them to be bad enough to refrain from committing them. On New Enlightenment principles—which on this matter most people apply even when they do not spell them out—what went on in Auschwitz was extremely bad, in that it caused untold suffering to the inmates and had a brutalizing effect on the perpetrators. It was all done moreover on the basis of a racial theory that is demonstrably false (few historical judgments are less dubious, than that the Jews have by and large done much more for humanity than most other races). On the basis of a consistent postmodernism (if that last expression is not an oxymoron), the claim that what went on in Auschwitz was bad is no better founded than the judgment that it was harmless or good.

50. See pp. 103, 115–16 below.

One might protest that the New Enlightenment is just one more pretext for Western cultural chauvinism. I do not see why this should be so. On some matters Western culture may well have, and in my view certainly does have, characteristic blind spots, due to inattention to evidence and failure to envisage possibilities ("scientism" is a notorious collection of such blind spots). The observations and insights enshrined in other cultures could provide useful correctives to these, and I believe actually do so.

It must be acknowledged here and now that there is one serious drawback to the New Enlightenment; the nature and grounds of this will be expounded in due course.

Note: The view suggested, but apparently rejected, by Plato in the *Theaetetus,*[51] that knowledge is true belief backed up by reasons, is supported by these considerations. In matters of science and in most matters of common sense, the "reasons" ultimately come down to sense experience; in matters of epistemology and metaphysics, to our experience of our own mental acts and the fact that the contradictories of the true propositions to be established imply propositions that are incompatible with their being intelligently conceived and reasonably affirmed. A sophisticated epistemologist might object that the examples adduced by Edmund Gettier,[52] as well as the famous hypothesis that we are "brains in vats," show that the account I have given is untenable. To answer these objections, one needs to make an addition to the formula: "By being rational, we come to know about a world which exists prior to and independently of ourselves." This addition might be formulated as follows:

51. 201d–210d.

52. "Is Justified True Belief Knowledge?" *Analysis* 23, no. 6 (1963), 121-23. For a discussion of the Gettier examples, see J. Dancy, *Contemporary Epistemology* (Oxford: Blackwell, 1985), 25–29.

". . . short of deliberate and thoroughgoing deception, and so long as the evidence is 'relevant' in every case to the proposition being reasonably asserted on the basis of it." Descartes' deceiving demon, and the mad scientist who has made us as brains and put us in vats, are authors of such deceptions. "Relevant" is to be defined in relation to Gettier-type examples. An object, say a mauve powder-puff, might appear to be in a place because of an elaborate arrangement of mirrors; and yet such an object might actually be in the place where one appears to be. In this case, the appearance that leads to the rational supposition that there is a real mauve powder-puff in a certain place, turns out, through a more sustained exercise of rationality, not to be *due to* the presence of a powder-puff in that place, even though one is actually there. It is in this sense that the evidence has to be "relevant" to the fact it is supposed to establish for Plato's formula to apply; and it is just this "relevance" which is missing in the Gettier examples.

3

POSTMODERNISM I

FOUCAULT AND DERRIDA

THE WORK of both Michel Foucault and Jacques Derrida is dominated by the conviction that "Western rationality" has somehow gone profoundly wrong. In *Madness and Civilization,*[1] Foucault commends Montaigne's opinion, that anyone who would ignore unreasonableness, and make their own reason the measure of everything, would themselves be unreasonable. As Foucault sees it, Renaissance intellectuals were never sure that they were not mad, and the medieval respect for astrologers and magicians persisted into their time. Mad people were only one group among many who testified to the fact that reason had its limits; it was acknowledged that their stories should be listened to, and that their secrets were worth hearing. Such views were, however, anathema to René Descartes, who may be regarded as more responsible than any other single person for the tearing apart of reason and unreason that is so characteristic of modernity. In his attempt to set reason on an abso-

1. *Histoire de la Folie* (Paris: Gallimard, 1972; originally published 1961). Translated as *Madness and Civilization* by Richard Howard (London: Tavistock Publications, 1967).

lutely secure foundation, Descartes supposed the existence of a malign and all-powerful demon, which was doing its best to deceive him.[2] For Foucault, it is reason itself that is the deceiving demon. And it is evident enough, as Roy Boyne remarks, that if we take seriously his efforts to counteract the demon's baneful influence, this will have tremendous repercussions on how we think and conduct our lives. As to our modern conceptions of mental illness, Foucault maintains that they make no sense except as contrasted with a reason that is supposed to be the ultimate arbiter of what is so and what is not so.[3]

Foucault seems to fear that reason as such is necessarily committed to exclusion. *Madness and Civilization* may be said to aspire to a form of discourse that is reasonable but not exclusivist; but in Foucault's later work, from about 1969 onwards, the hope that a different form of reasoning might in future be instituted seems to have evaporated. All the same, Foucault's work has won a great deal of attention from those who are critical of modern society. This is because, in spite of the increasing pessimism of his thought (at least until its very last phase), he drew attention throughout his work to those who have been marginalized by society and the processes by which they have been so.[4]

In his critique of *Madness and Civilization,* which evidently exerted a profound influence on Foucault, Derrida points out that all the documents cited by Foucault in support of his own case must, in virtue of the fact that they communicate meaning at all, be implicated in reason. And reason can be exercised only through exclusion. It seems that Foucault wants to bring

2. *Meditations on First Philosophy,* II.

3. See Roy Boyne, *Foucault and Derrida. The Other Side of Reason* (London: Unwin Hyman, 1990), 43, 44, 53. In my summary of the views of Foucault and Derrida, I depend heavily on Boyne's admirably compact and useful book, though I disagree with most of his conclusions.

4. Boyne, *Foucault,* 54, 61, 65.

a historical guilt to light and to put it on trial. However, as Derrida says, "such a trial may be impossible, for by the simple fact of their articulation the proceedings and the verdict unceasingly reiterate the crime."[5] It really makes no sense to postulate, as Foucault does, a higher type of reason than the one that we already acknowledge. Further, any attempt to counteract reason must itself lie within the ambit of reason. "The unsurpassable, unique and imperial grandeur of the order of reason, that which makes it not just another actual order or structure (a determined historical structure, one structure among other possible ones), is that one cannot speak out against it except by being for it, that one can protest it only from within; and within its domain. Reason leaves us only the recourse to stratagems and strategies."[6] As to the diremption of reason from unreason, as Derrida sees the matter, Foucault was wrong to place it as late as the seventeenth century; it was established at least as early as Plato. Indeed, to suppose that it occurred at any particular time commits one to postulating "an event or a structure subsequent to the unity of an original presence"[7]—which itself, as we shall see, is a cardinal error so far as Derrida is concerned.[8]

What apparently annoys Derrida most about "Western rationality"—in spite of the pervasive sense of outrage conveyed by his writings, his motives for this are not obvious—is, as Boyne suggests, its arrogance and its unfounded certitude. Derrida is

5. Jacques Derrida, " 'Cogito' and the History of Madness," in *Writing and Difference* (London: Routledge, 1978), 35.

6. Derrida, " 'Cogito,' " 36. According to Jonathan Culler, the deconstructive critic is "in a position not of sceptical detachment but of unwarrantable involvement" (*On Deconstruction. Theory and Criticism after Structuralism* [Ithaca, N.Y.: Cornell University Press, 1982], 88). This is because exercises in deconstruction "do not escape the logocentric premises they undermine; and there is no reason to believe that a theoretical enterprise could ever free itself from those premises" (7). The unregenerate may be tempted to comment that, if involvement is unwarrantable, then one should not get involved.

7. Derrida, " 'Cogito,' " 40.

8. Boyne, *Foucault,* 57–60, 63–64.

famous for his polemics against "the metaphysics of presence," and for his "deconstruction" of the "hierarchical oppositions" that are supposed to derive from it. What is to be made of these notions? What the "metaphysics of presence" may most plausibly be said to amount to, is the assumption that we might somehow apprehend reality directly, and without any distorting medium. In these ideal circumstances, it is supposed, the world would be immediately present to the human subject, who could at that moment speak of what she saw. This dream of ideal presence, which also underlies natural science, is conspicuous in Plato, to whose work, it has rightly been said, all subsequent Western philosophy consists of footnotes. In the myth of the cave in Book VII of his *Republic,* Plato writes of the journey from darkness into light, a light in which beauty, goodness, and justice would be immediately *present* to the beholder. In the *Phaedrus,* again, Plato envisages "a memory with no sign,"[9] which is in direct contact with truth and wisdom. In Derrida's view, this assumption about an original presence gives rise to most of the elements of traditional metaphysics; for example, "presence of the object to sight as eidos, presence as substance/essence/existence (ousia), . . . self-presence of the cogito, consciousness, subjectivity." "Logocentrism," as obsession with reason or the word within the history of Western thought, is "bound up in the determination of the being of the existent as present."[10]

Another key example for Derrida's purposes is Edmund Husserl's phenomenology, with its avowed attempt to know in an unmediated manner the true nature of things. In his *Logical Investigations,* Husserl makes a distinction between *expression* and *indication,* and he argues that, in the case of silently talking

9. "Plato's Pharmacy," in Derrida, *Dissemination* (London: Athlone Press, 1981), 109.

10. Derrida, *Of Grammatology* (Baltimore: Johns Hopkins University Press, 1976), 12; Culler, *Deconstruction,* 92–93.

to oneself, one "expresses" what is completely and immediately present to consciousness, so no "indication" is involved. As Boyne puts Derrida's position on the matter, "there is . . . , for Husserl, an imagined moment, prior to the arrival of language, when meaning and consciousness are fully present to each other. But, and this is the crucial point, this is a moment which we can never know." So far as Derrida is concerned, what Plato and Husserl have in common with the Western tradition in general is a disparagement of what is *supplementary* to the original "presence."[11] Among the most important consequences of this prejudice is a devaluation of writing as opposed to speech.

"Structuralists" like Jacques Lacan and Claude Levi-Strauss argued (taking a tip from the linguistics of Ferdinand Saussure) that meaning is produced by a system of signifiers, not signifiers one by one. (Thus "dog" is able to mean *dog* by virtue of its differences from "dot," "cog," "dig," and so on, rather than because of anything in the collocation of sounds or written marks "dog" in itself.) Derrida infers from this that the sound present at the moment of utterance "is inhabited by traces of the forms one is not uttering, and it can function as signifier only insofar as it consists of such traces." Evidently the same applies to writing as to speech; "each 'element', phoneme or grapheme—is constituted with reference to the trace in it of the forms one is not uttering, and it can be a signifier only insofar as it consists of such traces of other elements of the sequence or system. . . . Nothing, either in the elements or in the system, is anywhere simply present or absent. There are only, everywhere, differences and traces of traces."[12] As Derrida sees it, structuralism was still dominated by the "metaphysics of presence," and the tyranny of reason continued to exert its

11. Cf. Derrida, *Dissemination,* 167. Boyne, *Foucault,* 90–94, 96–97.
12. Derrida, *Positions,* 26. Cf. Culler, *Deconstruction,* 100.

power through notions like that of absolute truth. Furthermore, as Boyne puts it, "the availability of the fundaments of the world (whether substances, essences, structures or subjects) was taken as unproblematic. Structuralism . . . made no difference to the deep but self-deceptive assumption of Western reason that the original source of reality could be recovered in its full integrity, with neither loss because of, nor distortion through the representative medium."[13] Derrida has two methods for dissolving this dream of reason. He describes and denounces the role that it has played in various classical texts of philosophy, and he celebrates marginal texts that have glimpsed something of its underlying error—like contemporary experimental writing, avant-garde poetry, and some of the works of Nietzsche. As to why the dream is fantasy rather than realistic achievement or aspiration, Derrida can show this only in particular instances—for which he cites texts in philosophy, psychoanalysis, and linguistics. For reasons already mentioned, he admits that he cannot criticize reason at a general level, so he confines himself to local skirmishes against its particular manifestations.[14]

On the basis of Derrida's critique of "presence," and of the notion that representation is secondary and ultimately inessential, a polemic may be mounted against all the opposite pairs of terms so characteristic of Western thought, such as those between "intelligible and sensible, inside and outside, good and evil, truth and falsehood, . . . nature and culture, man and woman," and so on. As seen in terms of Derrida's critique of presence, these are "not simple alternatives. It is rather the case that one side of each opposition has a presumed privilege over

13. Derrida is said to criticize structuralism most notably in an essay of 1971, "The supplement of the copula: philosophy before linguistics," in *Margins of Philosophy* (Brighton: Harvester Press, 1982) 175–205. Boyne, *Foucault,* 106.

14. Boyne, *Foucault,* 91, 105–6.

the other. One side is original, the other side secondary, derivative, worth less."[15] In Western thinking, difference brings with it absence of value. What is different is found threatening and beyond comprehension; its alien otherness eludes the control of those persons who are well established within social hierarchies. One tends to cope with it by either neutralizing or incorporating it. However, one may instead aspire to a way of thinking that invites and affirms such differences. Boyne suggests that Derrida's thinking bears usefully on these matters, because he shows how little ground there is for the hierarchies that control us, often hurting and wounding us in so doing. Possibly some such hierarchies are necessary at our present stage of social development, but we have no reason to suppose that other kinds of arrangement are not in principle possible.[16]

Both Foucault and Derrida insist on the recognition and affirmation of difference. The metaphysics of presence, by contrast, in Boyne's words, "does not tolerate difference unless it is accompanied by deference." Thus the inferiority and derivativeness of writing is played off against the purity and originality of speech;[17] culture is denigrated as falsifying and corrupting nature; emotion and intuition are dismissed in favor of the claims of rationality. So we have "a general situation in which a full, present and powerful plenitude sustains its privileged position by parasitically sucking the life out of that upon which the myth of this power, presence, and all-consuming adequacy is imposed. . . . In each case a judgement is made by a self-appointed superior over a presumed inferior, and the judgement is *always* that the qualities of the inferior are *in every respect*

15. Ibid., 125. Cf. Derrida, *Limited Inc.* (Baltimore: Johns Hopkins University Press, 1977), 66; Culler, *Deconstruction,* 93.

16. Boyne, *Foucault,* 124.

17. This of course is a central theme of *Of Grammatology.* Cf. also Derrida, *Dissemination,* 158; and Culler, *Deconstruction,* 89.

inadequate and derivative copies of the superior instance. This is the story and process which deconstruction seeks to challenge."[18]

It is evident enough that the considerations raised so far make the notion of truth, in the sense of a representation of things as they really are, highly problematic. As Boyne expresses Derrida's view: "What is truth except a representation of the truth; and because representation is . . . an inferior substitution which might also be a false substitution, who is to say that *this* is the truth? . . . Whosoever claims the truth, claims to reveal it in the glory of its full presence, claims to mime it with utter faithfulness, must be a magician. For it is only a strictly magical ability, a hypnotic talent, a supreme cleverness that can persuade us that what we have seen is the light rather than its reflection, the presence rather than its representation."[19] One obvious corollary is the denial that "the real events of history can be unproblematically *presented* by an historical text . . . this recognition of the essential absence at the heart of the text will force Derrida to be critical of the very notion of history itself." Similarly, one may see Foucault's "archaeology of knowledge" as an attack on history as conceived in a rationalist manner, and as a consequence on the conceptions of historical truth and objectivity. As to Foucault's scepticism, one of its casualties is the traditional conception of the conscious subject. If we follow his suggestions in "A Preface to Transgression,"[20] we have to wonder how far "the subject" and related notions can retain their validity. As he says, "the breakdown of philosophical subjectivity . . . is probably one of the fundamental structures of contemporary

18. Boyne, *Foucault,* 135; my italics.

19. Ibid., 97. Derrida remarks that the apparent "effacement of the signifier" in speech, which is a main target of deconstruction, is "the condition of the very idea of truth" (*Grammatology,* 20).

20. In *Language, Counter-Memory, Practice,* ed. Donald Bouchard (Oxford: Blackwell, 1977).

thought."[21] What is at issue here is what has been called "the death of the subject"; it is a consequence of the fact that the thought of the (old) Enlightenment was capable of encompassing every conceivable object but one—the subject of thought herself. "It is at the centre of the subject's disappearance," Foucault writes, "that philosophical language proceeds as though through a labyrinth, not to recapture him but to test the extremity of its loss."[22] He answers Derrida's suggestion, that a language other than that of reason is impossible, by remarking that reason as we know it is invariably based on oppositions such as that of object and subject, same and other, but that these oppositions may be falling apart.[23]

Let us ask what, in the light of the principles of the New Enlightenment, it is to submit "oppositions," whether "hierarchical" or otherwise, to critical examination. One has first to distinguish sharply the "hierarchical" contrasts from those which are not hierarchical, the evaluative from the nonevaluative, and to apply all these sets of contrasts with as much rationality (attentiveness, intelligence, and reasonableness) as possible. In doing so, we should be particularly on the lookout for bias due to our personal or group interests. Some contrasts (between sexual debauchery of young children and love and care for them, between murdering people with axes and feeding them when they are hungry) are really matters of value; others, which are not (female as opposed to male, black human being as opposed to white) tend to slide into being so. To be rational and responsible is to be on the lookout for this happening, not only in the thought, speech and action of other individuals and

21. "Preface," 42. David Kolb writes of "the postmodern claim that we have no unified self to collect" (*Postmodern Sophistications* [Chicago and London: University of Chicago Press, 1990], 36).

22. "Preface," 43.

23. Boyne, *Foucault,* 79, 83–84, 86, 97.

groups, but rather especially in one's own. And when this slide is found to have occurred, one should clarify, by attention to the basic norms of truth and goodness, how far this serves as a pretext for errors founded on self- or group-interest. (It was convenient for whites of the southern United States, in the early nineteenth century, to separate the children of black slaves from their parents at a very early age; so the false theory was put about, in order to make the practice appear less cruel than it was, that blacks by nature had less strong family attachments than whites.)[24]

On the philosophical principles of the New Enlightenment, as well as (one would have thought) in accordance with elementary common sense, to be rational about such contrasts or "oppositions" is neither to accept them just as they are, nor totally to jettison them. It is to ask how far they tend to foster, and how far to obstruct, the knowing of what is true, and the knowing and doing of what is good. Where differences between individuals and groups within societies are concerned, one has to ask which differences can be allowed, or even encouraged, to flourish, and which should be discouraged or even forbidden as leading to undue suffering, frustration, unfairness, or curtailment of freedom. Some "differences," like those between females and males, architects and lawyers,[25] black persons and white, should presumably not on the whole be accompanied by "deference";[26] others, like those between cruelty and kindness, the evasion of truth and the pursuit of it, the toadying to tyranny

24. See Samuel Eliot Morison, *The Oxford History of the American People* (New York: Oxford University Press, 1965), 507.

25. Though the lawyer will be wise usually to defer to the architect on matters architectural, and vice versa. Also it is arguable that whites should show special, but not excessively special, consideration toward members of other races, due to sensitivities arising from past abuses. The same, I believe, applies to the dealings of men with women, and of women with men.

26. Boyne, *Foucault,* 135.

and injustice and the resistance to or denunciation of them, certainly ought to be so. In other cases still of difference, like that between parents and young children, teachers and their students, brain surgeons and their assistants, there should presumably be some deference, at least within a limited area of interaction, and always against a background of mutual respect. Certainly those who wear garish ties in public places, however much they may happen to annoy a few of their more soberly attired fellow-citizens, ought not to be subjected to restraints or reprisals; but the same can hardly apply to rapists, child-abusers, or mass murderers.

In short, it is absurd from the point of view of common sense, let alone from that of the New Enlightenment, to maintain that all differences should either be universally recognized and encouraged, in the manner apparently recommended by both Foucault and Derrida, or universally assimilated or marginalized, as they claim is implied by "Western rationality." The fact is that some differences are, and are universally in practice recognized to be, matters of value and such that the better should be encouraged, the worse counteracted or resisted. To be properly rational is to ask what differences truly are matters of value and what are not, and what differences it is feasible, in the light of the overall good, to allow to flourish. How much freedom of expression, for example, can be permitted, when some people want to express hatred of racial or cultural minorities? The opinion appears to be steadily gaining ground that homosexuals should not be discriminated against on the grounds of the practices natural to their sexual orientation; the reason for this is that it appears that the cessation of such discrimination tends greatly to increase the happiness of the substantial proportion of the population who are homosexual, without harming or distressing the heterosexual majority to any great extent. But it would be quite a different matter similarly to leave to their own devices habitual murderers, embezzlers or child-molesters.[27]

The acknowledgment of some differences, of value and otherwise, tends to be corroborated by the comprehensive rationality of the New Enlightenment, as representing the truth and contributing to the overall good of humankind; that of others, not. There are real differences between women and men, white persons and black; there are also real differences between intelligence and stupidity, malevolence and good intention. What will not do is to assume as a matter of course that men are always more intelligent than women, or for that matter women more sensitive than men; or that blacks are congenitally more benevolent than whites, or vice versa. Rationality, on the Old Enlightenment as well as the New Enlightenment model, brings out the absurdity or monstrousness of such assumptions; to insist, as Foucault and Derrida often seem to do, that "Western rationality" as such is somehow committed to them, is palpably wrong-headed. But whatever is to blame for them, it should scarcely be necessary to add that, on the New Enlightenment view, the cure for such debilitating prejudices is *more* rationality, not *less.*

Certainly, when people urge us, as Foucault and Derrida may be supposed to do, to question how far the structures of hierarchy and authority in society foster overall happiness, freedom and justice, and how far they are apt rather to hurt, wound, or frustrate people, it is worth attending to them. But within a New Enlightenment perspective, as from the point of view of common sense, it would seem, at first sight at least, that some types of hierarchy and authority are beneficent in their overall effect, however harmful others may be. I may feel irked when the police stop me for speeding, but no sane person doubts that

27. Cf. Foucault's chilling remark about the consent of children to sexual practices, cited on p. 89 below.

speed limits are a good thing overall, or that some officials are needed to enforce them. In a hospital, it is a good thing that a brain surgeon should be able to give orders and expect them to be obeyed; otherwise, too many patients will die or be turned into vegetables. In a university department of engineering, again, it is no bad thing that the opinions of the professors that are of relevance to their specialty should on the whole have more authority than those of students who are new to the subject, and that the professors should be able to grade the performance of the students in a way that has some bearing on their subsequent careers; otherwise buildings and bridges will be rather more liable to collapse than they are at present, with a good deal of pain, maiming, and loss of life as a result. (Some postmodernists have the bad habit of hinting that in a distant future, which we cannot now clearly envisage, things might be quite otherwise.[28] The charm of such suggestions appears to me directly proportionate to one's failure to think them through.)

In short, a generalized "deconstruction" of "hierarchical oppositions," so far as one can get a clear view of what it would actually amount to, seems worse than useless for practical purposes, as compared to rational investigation of them with a view to the true and the good. I am afraid that I myself believe—and Foucault and Derrida show in some contexts that they themselves effectively believe—that the true should be privileged over the false, the good over the bad. Deconstruction may have its uses, so far as it leads some people to consider carefully whether what they assume to be true or good is actually to be confirmed as being such by stringent and unbiassed investigation; and to wonder whether their own race, class, or gender is really better than others in quite all the respects that it suits them to assume. But this desirable end will be achieved much more effectively by investigation that is "rational" in the sense that I have described,

28. Cf. p. 62 above.

than by deconstruction, which, on the most obvious interpretation at least, is just as destructive of the norms that I have described as of those which are less fundamental.

On New Enlightenment principles, the commendable opinion that the true and the good should be privileged over the false and the bad is sharply to be distinguished from the view that the convictions of one's own group, or the group that happens to be most privileged in one's society, should be promulgated by any means available, and all others ridiculed or misrepresented. Suppressed and marginalized persons and groups are likely to have undergone experiences and grasped possibilities that have been neglected by more fortunate ones, especially in relation to those matters where the latter have a vested interest in concealing the truth from others and from themselves. For example, some of those called "insane" by the conventionally "rational" may well have beliefs that a more thoroughgoing rationality would confirm as closer to the truth; I take it that this is the point of Montaigne's paradoxical remark that it is unreasonable to ignore unreasonableness. R. D. Laing and others have shown how it is often the member of a family who is stigmatized as "mentally ill" whose assessment of what is going on in that family is closest to the mark, and how it is the uncomfortable nature of that assessment which renders it unacceptable as a serious possibility by other family members.[29] The point seems to have more general application to the acquisition of knowledge. Edward de Bono once remarked, in the course of a discussion, that he thought a schizophrenic and an engineer would make the ideal team of scientific discoverers—the schizophrenic thinking up possibilities that no one had thought of before, the engineer testing the possibilities one by one. Of the components of rationality as conceived by the New Enlighten-

29. Cf. *The Divided Self* (Harmondsworth: Penguin Books, 1969) and *The Families of Schizophrenics* (London: Tavistock, 1970).

ment, the schizophrenic of course represents intelligence, the engineer reasonableness.

There *is* something important to be learned, from the point of view of the New Enlightenment, from Derrida's critique of "presence," though it is not exactly what Derrida and his followers have actually inferred from it. Immediate experience merely gives us *clues to* the real world, which itself can be known only through the medium of judgment based on understanding. And by this means also, as I have already briefly argued, we can gain an ever fuller apprehension of goodness, justice, and so on. On this view, Plato's particular account of our apprehension of these ideals—as "seen" directly with the eyes of the mind in an earlier life—is better taken as a potent myth than an accurate account of how things are. And yet it does seem that we can get a more or less clear sense of ideals, which operate, and necessarily operate, in all our thought, by the kind of procedure which I have already described. By being thoroughly rational, and by reflecting rationally on our rationality, we can get an ever clearer idea of what it is to come to know what is true and good, and to act accordingly. If denial of this fact, rather than merely rejection of this or that way of expressing it, is implied by Derrida's polemics against the "metaphysics of presence," then his views are to that extent in error, and dangerously so, unless my own arguments about the matter have been unsound.

Derrida seems to argue in effect[30] that talk of "origins" is systematically misleading, and that appeal to "nature" or what is "natural" is always or at least usually a cloak for ideology. But for all his apparent disclaimers, there is surely rather good reason to believe that we as human beings, and indeed as the particular individuals that we are, are originally and naturally endowed,

30. The vagueness of this phraseology is deliberate; it seems of the essence of the Derridean enterprise that one cannot draw out clear implications or applications from Derrida's claims and arguments.

due to divine gift or evolutionary inheritance or both, with certain potentialities or predispositions, which our physical, cultural, and social environment may more or less fulfil, to our long-term satisfaction and that of our fellow human beings, or frustrate, with unhappiness or suffering as the result. These potentialities and limitations are what are most usefully designated as the human, or our own individual, "essence" or "nature." In *Mythologies,* Roland Barthes rightly maintains that it is characteristic of ideology to produce "natural-seemingness."[31] For example, if one race or sex happened to be subordinated to another within some society, such subordination might be assumed there to be "natural" owing to the alleged mental or moral superiority of the privileged group, without there being any objective evidence in favor of this. The New Enlightenment would ask what in such human arrangements *is* really natural, and what merely seems to be so due to the influence of ideology. One might profitably raise such a question, for example, about the supposed need of steady relationships with particular adults for healthy psychological development in children;[32] or the alleged disposition of young women on the whole to gain greater sexual satisfaction from men with whom they have a close personal tie than from comparative strangers.[33]

It looks as though each of us has a unique version of the human essence in the sense of the term that I have suggested, due to biological inheritance, personal history, overall situation in life, and so on.[34] Some people are probably not at all suited

31. Boyne, *Foucault,* 105–6.

32. Cf. John Bowlby, *Child Care and the Growth of Love* (Harmondsworth: Penguin Books, 1953).

33. Cf. Donald Symons, *The Evolution of Human Sexuality* (Oxford: Oxford University Press, 1979), 219.

34. Plato, *Republic,* Books IV and V; cf. A. E. Taylor, *Plato. The Man and His Work* (London: Methuen 1960), 275–76. C. G. Jung, *Psychological Types* (London: Kegan Paul, 1923); David Keirsey and Marilyn Bates, *Please Understand Me. Character and Temperament Types* (Del Mar, Calif.: Prometheus

to being academic professors, others to being firefighters or purveyors of Greek wine. It is worth noting in this connection that—short of some assumptions about human potentialities, whether universal or particular or both, which may be taken as given, and about how they may be more or less realized or frustrated—all policies for revolution or reform that are other than arbitrary are scuttled from the start. For must not every revolutionary or reformer claim, at least implicitly, that her cause is good? But what could this claim amount to, other than that its implementation would fulfil human potentialities more adequately than the presently established economic, social, or political arrangements?[35] And surely it is a matter of common sense, strongly confirmed by behavioral science, that the influences on persons, particularly in the early stages of life, could be changed in such a way that all or most people would be more likely than they are at present both to find fulfilment for themselves and to be able and willing to act for the fulfilment of others and so for the general good. If Foucault or Derrida would deny, as they sometimes appear to do, that we have sufficient cognitive and moral self-transcendence to envisage and work for a physical and social environment that is better in this kind of way, they are just wrong. If they were right, social "progress," as opposed to arbitrary change, would be rendered impossible, in fact inconceivable.

Certainly, "the availability of the fundaments of the world and human nature (whether substances, essences, structures or

---

Nemesis, 1984). The last two differ from the first in having no hierarchical suggestion: each type of character is complementary to the others, all are equally needed for the functioning of society, and none is intrinsically superior or inferior to the others.

35. Some authorities, notably Louis Althusser in *For Marx* (Harmondsworth: Penguin Books, 1969), think that the concept of alienation plays no part in Marx's mature thought. For the definitive refutation of this thesis, see David McLellan, *The Thought of Karl Marx. An Introduction* (London: Macmillan 1971), 108–10.

subjects)" should not be "taken as unproblematic,"[36] and "Western rationality" in its Old Enlightenment form is to be criticized so far as it does so. Like everything else, this availability should be questioned, according to the New Enlightenment. But in fact such questioning seems to establish it more firmly, confirming that there are "substances" or individuals, that I exist, that my cat, my house and my piano do so, and that we are all distinct from one another. It can be similarly established that each of these beings has a number of characteristics, short of which it would neither exist nor be what it is. These may reasonably be called its "essence." Furthermore, this world appears to be characterized by structure as well as by chaos and to consist of what is lawful as well as what is due merely to the vagaries of chance, or we would not be able to know about it or operate within it as we do. Lastly, there would appear really to exist "subjects," entities, like myself, my reader, Foucault, the King of Norway, and Derrida, who are capable of acting, speaking, and thinking in a more or less rational manner. All these things, if questioned, can be established on the basis of the New Enlightenment principles I have sketched. Now I have argued that "the actual world" or "reality" can be nothing other than what we tend to form judgments about so far as we are as rational as possible. Yet it has been said of Derrida that he regards it as a "deep but self-deceptive assumption of Western reason" that we might apprehend reality "with neither loss because of, nor distortion through the representational medium."[37] But *this* is to assume what I have already argued is false: that reality might somehow be different in the last analysis from what would be "represented" at the ideal limit by the "representational medium" constituted by well-founded or rational human judgment.

It appears to me to be a mistake to treat "Western rationality" as unique in kind from a cultural point of view; rather, science

36. Boyne, *Foucault,* 106. 37. Ibid.

and democracy, if the New Enlightenment is right, result from the thorough application, to a very wide range of problems, of principles that seem to be of the essence of all human thought and language. However "primitive" a human society, its members will have to be to some extent attentive, intelligent, reasonable, and responsible for it to survive. They will have to be attentive to sensory clues, and intelligently and reasonably infer from them the poisonousness of berries or the proximity of man-eating tigers; every now and then someone will have responsibly to sacrifice her own interests to those of the group. And historical experience shows that, for all the ills attendant on representative democracy, it is probably the least unsatisfactory of all known forms of government. As to the problems that afflict "science" and "democracy" here and now, they are to be solved by more and not less rationality. It is the opposite of "rational" to be so obsessed with technology that we deplete the earth's natural resources or are no longer able to enjoy the beauty of unspoiled nature. Technological sophistication is one means of realizing the human good; but it is the opposite of "rational" to think that it is the only means.

From the point of view of the New Enlightenment, Foucault's attack on "Western rationality" seems partly incoherent, partly indicative of real defects in the Old Enlightenment, at least as this is often conceived and implemented. Descartes, who is representative par excellence of the Old Enlightenment, is notorious as having stressed those aspects of the acquisition of knowledge which are a matter of construing the world in terms of deductive system, and as having underestimated the role of experience and creative hypothesis. According to the New Enlightenment, what is basically involved in the acquisition of knowledge is attention to experience, creative hypothesizing, and reasonable affirmation of those judgments which are corroborated by one's experience. Certainly, explanation of all the data is to be aimed for; but this need not necessarily be a matter of rigorous deduction. (To explain why you *went* to lunch when you did, is not necessarily to explain why you *could not but have gone* to lunch when you did; and the same seems to apply to the particular instant at which a radioactive atom, by emitting a particle, becomes an atom of a different element.) Now excluded judgments, whether those of one sex, or of an underprivileged race or class, may well be based on experiences and hypotheses that have been overlooked, or even more or less deliberately suppressed, by those in power. As Foucault and Derrida both bring out with considerable force, a set of factual or value judgments may prevail in a society or group, not because they constitute the most reasonable set of hypotheses to explain the available evidence, but because they suit the interests or self-image of the most influential members of it. The truth may well look crazy, or at least worth dismissing as crazy, to those who have investment in a status quo that depends on ignorance of it. Unfortunately, it is characteristic of the patrons of both postmodernism and deconstruction that their norms, or lack of norms, are destructive of any coherent notion of truth and any means by which truth might be known. And yet they ineluctably depend upon a notion of truth, and assumptions about how it may at least in principle be known, by the very fact that they hold the opinions they do and expect others to take them seriously.

In his critique of Foucault's *Madness and Civilization,* Derrida seems within an ace of advancing to the viewpoint of the New Enlightenment, when he points out that one cannot coherently attack reason without depending on reason to do so.[38] Surely the proper outcome of this insight would have been to distinguish those elements of the Old Enlightenment, or "Western rationality," which represent genuine and comprehensive rationality (attentiveness, intelligence, and reasonableness, with

38. See pp. 57–58 above.

all their implications) from those which do not. Such comprehensive rationality of course by no means—quite the contrary—rules out a wide envisagement of possibilities, including some that conventional or lazy people, or those hidebound by restricted or incoherent notions of "rationality," would be liable to dismiss as absurd or even insane. Indeed, a genuine New Enlightenment rationality will be disposed to give special attention to possibilities which the prejudices of the powerful might give them strong motives to dismiss or to overlook—typically, those entertained by despised or marginalized groups. To revert to the terminology of the New Enlightenment, one has to have been intelligent in order to be reasonable, to have envisaged a range of possibilities before one is in a position to determine which of these is likely to be the case.

However, once one comes to the level of reasonableness, it has to be admitted that judgment as such does exclude. This is the burden of Aristotle's principle of noncontradiction.[39] It cannot both be the case and be not the case that I am sitting here and now in a room in Calgary writing the first draft of this sentence; that water both is and is not a chemical compound; that the land mass of Greenland is at once larger than and smaller than that of Iceland; that the torture of babies for fun is at once sometimes permissible and never permissible. Every determination is a negation, as the Scholastic tag has it. But it will not do, for all that it is a regular practice on the part of both Foucault and Derrida, to assimilate the kind of exclusion that is intrinsic to reasonable judgment of fact or value on the one hand, to the thoughtless and vicious exclusions of persons based on sexual orientation, gender, wealth or whatever on the other. Indeed, the value judgment, "it would be a good thing on balance to take the judgments of the so-called insane more seriously than we have done up to now," excludes the contra-

39. *Metaphysics,* Gamma, 4.

dictory judgment that this would *not* on balance be a good thing.

According to the epistemology of the New Enlightenment, as I have already argued at some length, we can have a coherent and practical account of the human good, of what it is badly to fall short of it, and what to approximate to it. Consequently, there is no good reason to submit to the thoroughgoing pessimism evinced by Foucault and Derrida throughout most of their careers. What I have called "moral self-transcendence" is after all possible; we can conceive of states of affairs that would be absolutely better or worse than the present circumstances for ourselves and others, where human life would be fairer and happier, and not merely according to criteria we just happen to have chosen, or that have been arbitrarily imposed on us by our society. And we can set ourselves to act accordingly. It is apparently quite difficult to conduct human affairs in a satisfactory way, but history shows that there have been better and worse shots at it, on the part of both individuals and societies. We can set ourselves in a more or less reasonable manner to change things in the direction of one and away from the other. Gradually, as our technology and our understanding of natural and social science advance, we can hope to become more adept at finding out what works relatively well and what does not. B. F. Skinner did well to deplore the fact that, though we can put human beings on the moon, we cannot as yet avoid constant violence in our inner cities and our schools.[40] But, whatever the deficiencies of Skinner's own proposed solutions to such problems, there is no reason why we should always be so helpless in coping with them.

Blanket condemnations of "Western rationality" are worse than useless if we are to rescue ourselves from our plight, especially when they aspire to "deconstruct" the "opposition" be-

40. *Beyond Freedom and Dignity* (London: Jonathan Cape, 1972), chap. 1.

tween what is good and what is bad. On the contrary, we have to determine what is really good and bad—in terms, as I have previously argued, of what contributes to happiness and fairness, and what has the opposite effect—and why the good things and the bad things tend to occur. We have to plan our actions and policies to secure the one and avoid the other. The sanest view about the changes brought about in our lives as a result of the Old Enlightenment is that they meet some of our needs while failing to meet others. We may properly enjoy our improved standard of living while being less than happy with what seems to accompany it—environmental pollution, bureaucratic control, and the rest of it. The surviving apologists for the Old Enlightenment try to restrict our attention constantly to the benefits, while the representatives of postmodernism rail against the evils. The most general practical question of the New Enlightenment is, how can we retain as many as possible of the former while avoiding the latter.

A fine example of useful reflection of this sort seems to be provided by Charles Handy's book *The Age of Paradox*,[41] which mentions a number of dilemmas that face us, and to which we do not yet know the solution. How are we to deal with the fact that there are people clamoring for work, and there is work crying out to be done—like cleaning up the environment and giving assistance to the elderly and infirm—yet the economic system somehow ensures that the two ends never meet? How do we achieve goods that are evidently more and more desirable to humankind at large—like a safe environment and unpolluted air—when there is no individual customer for them, and so organizations are not motivated to produce them?

As Peregrine Worsthorne wrote some years ago:

41. Cambridge, Mass.: Harvard Business School Press, 1994; see Peter Larson, "Modern Life Spawns Paradoxes," *Calgary Herald*, December 31, 1994, F7.

> No one knows how to make the great bulk of industrial work sufficiently interesting to engage the workers' enthusiastic co-operation, how to restore dignity to labour. No one knows how to control inflation without the cure causing more social turbulence than the disease. No one knows how to reshape and re-organize cities so as to recreate among their inhabitants any sense of civic pride and loyalty. No one knows how to get the balance right between industrial growth and natural amenity. No one knows how to industrialise under-developed countries without in the long run destroying the very markets needed by the West for its economic survival. No one knows how to reconcile the new opportunities for world-wide human mobility, greatly aggravated by population explosions, with the old racial antipathies which prevent assimilation of strangers, particularly where colour is involved.[42]

Even if there are no complete solutions to such dilemmas, there are presumably more and less satisfactory compromises in principle available to us. Worsthorne laments that one of the most persistent obstacles to clarifying the nature of, let alone solving, these problems, is the intergroup hatred that has bedevilled traditional politics. But perhaps an even more dangerous obstruction is the premature despair of reason encouraged by the sponsors of postmodernism.

Derrida's play with the contrast between speech and writing is another fair example of the way in which his mental acrobatics impede rather than facilitate clear insight into the human condition and how it might be changed for the better. I myself do not find, in the part of the historical record with which I am acquainted, much confirmation for his well-known claim that Western civilization has systematically devalued writing in favor of speech. Derrida's argument for this notorious thesis is not improved by his equivocation on the concept of writing, which

42. *Encounter,* vol. 52, no. 4, 12–13; quoting Worsthorne in *The Sunday Telegraph.*

sometimes appears to mean signification in general (which Derrida is apt unhelpfully to call "arche-writing"), and sometimes writing in the common or garden sense.[43] Insofar as Plato, Rousseau, Husserl, and others really did value speech over writing, it seems reasonanble to ask why they did so, and how far they were right in so doing. It is evident that writing has its positive uses as a supplement(!) to speech, to record contracts, to preserve the memory of what was said or done on some important occasion, and so on. Derrida excels in the baleful art of Procrustes; he first pillories Plato for starting the alleged "Western" habit of denigrating writing in favor of speech, and then he inveighs against him for admitting that writing after all has its worthwhile side. (At least it is not recorded of Procrustes that he *first* stretched his guests until they were too long for his bed, and *then* chopped off their extremities in order to make them short enough for it.) There is no doubt that writing, while presumably in some sense "supplementary" to speech, has been of enormous and indispensable benefit to civilization—without it, how could I enjoy the benefits of Derrida's reflections on matters of present concern? But it seems to have certain drawbacks as well, like a general decline in memory and oral creativity—Cecil Sharp and Ralph Vaughan Williams, at the beginning of the twentieth century, were only just in time to rescue from oblivion what was left of English folksong. The question for the New Enlightenment is how we can enjoy the best of the progress made possible by the fact that we have writing as well as speech, while mitigating as much as we can the sad losses that seem, as things are now, to be the inevitable consequence of it. The obscure reflections of Derrida on this subject, what-

43. Cf. also John Ellis's acid comment: "If we decide arbitrarily to call language 'writing', speech 'phonic', and writing 'graphic', we have not changed the relation of the three entities" (*Against Deconstruction* [Princeton, N.J.: Princeton University Press, 1989], 24).

ever they amount to, seem a positive hindrance to this vital task. Sophisticated trifling of the kind exemplified by his writings has its place in intellectual life, but is a menace so far as it distracts thinking people from the serious tasks of dispelling falsehood and illusion and making life more fulfilling for human beings.

As I have already mentioned, to judge by the principles of the New Enlightenment, there is something to be learned from Derrida's aspersions on the "metaphysics of presence." We do not directly and immediately confront reality, and there is no need to assume (following Plato's suggestion) that we did so in an earlier life. Direct experience—of the sound as of a violin playing low G, of visual sensations as though of a square yellow patch—does not yield reality itself so much as clues to it. As Lonergan remarks, "The Humean world of mere impressions comes to me as a puzzle to be pieced together."[44] We get at what *is* only through the medium of judgments framed in terms of concepts excogitated by intelligence, and these tend to be affected for the worse by our individual and social biases. Yet we can identify and work against these biases—by being as attentive, intelligent, and reasonable as we can—and so at least get closer to the truth about things. That our sense experience, and the experience of our feelings, as well as our awareness of the mental processes we apply to them in order to find out what is true about the world and what is good, are sufficiently "present" to us to provide reliable foundations for such knowledge, has already been argued. Whatever defects there may have been in their detailed solutions to the problem, Plato and Husserl were quite right in seeking for foundations for knowledge, and in supposing that such foundations are in principle knowable by us. Derrida dilates on the overweening conceit of "Western rationality" in supposing that it can apprehend reality, or

44. *Insight,* XI, 2.

even approach doing so, in a manner that is undistorted by the medium through which we apprehend it. Yet the charge may properly be turned against him; *he* apparently presupposes that he has some privileged access to reality, by the very fact that he thinks himself entitled to inveigh against "Western rationality" for failing to apprehend reality or even to be on the way toward doing so. He himself would have to have some conception of the real, to form a basis for his criticism of Western reason as being unable to grasp it. In general, the work of Foucault and Derrida, and that of all their innumerable followers, is shot through with the paradox that they implicitly presuppose what they explicitly deny—the hallmark of "counterpositions" in the New Enlightenment sense. They must do this, indeed, whenever they speak or write an indicative sentence, for such sentences are by their very nature expressions of judgment. As such they make claims about the "reality" to which they maintain we have no access. And what in the last analysis could "reality" be, other than that to which we tend to have access through our judgments so far as they are rational?

It is obvious that the whole of science, as indeed of common sense knowledge, depends on the assumption that we can in principle get at the truth about things, and so apparently on some form of the "metaphysics of presence." One wonders what the attitude of Foucault or Derrida is to such matters as the theory of evolution, the oxygen theory of combustion, or the existence of a giant planet outside the orbit of Uranus. Do they really think that there is in the last analysis no reason to suppose that the statements affirming these things to be the case are more likely to be true than their contradictories? That would seem to follow from Derrida's position, and indeed from that of Foucault, since they would both appear to deplore the rationality on which such putative items of knowledge are based. Just the same would apply to statements of fact of a common sense kind, as, that Jean-Paul Sartre was a prolific writer and fluent speaker of French, that General Charles de Gaulle was a taller man than the average, or that Jacques Derrida was alive and active in the ninth decade of the twentieth century.

Foucault and Derrida both eschew appeal to general principles in their criticism of reason; on their account, one can engage in polemic only against its particular manifestations. It seems to follow ineluctably from this that such polemics must be totally arbitrary. What could such "criticism" amount to, given that it was worth the name at all, without at least implicit appeal to a general principle or principles of some kind? One might indeed properly make a complaint against some actual or supposed manifestation of "Western reason," on the ground that it has restricted freedom of experience or the free play of understanding; but this, of course, would be a matter of appeal to a general principle. Also, as I have already shown, such restrictions could be imposed in the name of reason only as a result of a misunderstanding of its real nature, which *presupposes* rather than *rules out* the free range of experience and understanding in attending to relevant data and envisaging possibilities. As to polemics that are arbitrary and without principle, they are not to be taken seriously.

The doubts raised by Derrida and Foucault—as to whether history, or at least the "rationalist" sort of history, which tries to find out what actually happened in the past, is really possible—are a typical instance of the absurdities into which good minds are driven if they do not have recourse to concrete examples. Do they really wish to maintain, as would appear to follow from what they say, that there is no reliable means of establishing whether Abraham Lincoln, Mrs. Proudie, Ivan the Terrible, or Rupert Bear were in all probability historical or fictional characters? In accordance with the epistemology of the New Enlightenment, of course, there is no difficulty whatever in setting out the means: in each case, one attends to the available evidence, envisages possible explanations for it, and prefers the explanation that suits the evidence best—that there was no such individual as Rupert Bear, that there was such a person as Abraham Lincoln. As to the alleged "death of the subject," nothing better illustrates the manner in which incidental defects in the Old Enlightenment lead inexorably to their postmodern nemesis. The Old Enlightenment applied scientific method to the explanation of reality with unprecedented thoroughness, but did not advert sufficiently to the fact that this method cannot consistently be envisaged in such a way as to eliminate the authentic subjectivity necessary for its implementation. If human beings are exhaustively explainable as physical and chemical machines, they cannot really be attentive, intelligent, or reasonable at all; let alone enough to believe that they are mere physical and chemical machines because they have good reason to do so. But the epistemology of the New Enlightenment does not conceive of scientific method in such a way as to make it in principle eliminative of human authenticity; on the contrary, it founds scientific method on human authenticity as attentive, intelligent, reasonable, and responsible. When we are invited by Foucault and others to wonder how far "the subject" and related notions can retain their validity at all, we have to ask, who is talking, and to whom is the invitation being addressed? Short of subjects to make them, and at least supposed subjects to whom they may be made, there can be no invitations. These presuppose entities in principle capable of having experience, questioning their experience, enjoying hunches, marshalling evidence for and against them, and making judgments accordingly. The New Enlightenment adopts from Descartes the point that I cannot coherently think that I am not a thinker or argue that I am not an arguer. The subject does not disappear from a comprehensively critical philosophy, so there is no need to get lost in the labyrinth that results from its supposed disappearance. As to Foucault's suggestion that the oppositions of subject and object, same and other, may now be falling apart—I can have as good reason as could possibly be for judging that my environment contains mere objects and other persons who are different from myself, like Foucault and my cousin Kitty, my refrigerator and the Eiffel Tower, which are distinct from me and from other subjects or objects. Philosophical reflection certainly makes the objects of naive realism problematic, but it can replace them with the objects and subjects of New Enlightenment critical realism, which are what are to be known by reason based on experience and understanding.

The fact is that the extreme scepticism flirted with by Foucault and Derrida is not only absurd at the practical level, but, as the epistemology of the New Enlightenment shows, quite unnecessary at the theoretical. And of course, as Derrida frequently admits in his own case, both authors constantly assume implicitly what they explicitly doubt or deny. Thus the whole of Derrida's criticism of Plato or Rousseau assumes that truth in history and interpretation is available—that Plato really wrote this or that, and that what he really meant by it can be established with a certain degree of reliability.

The mischievous effect of Derridean deconstruction, if one wishes to learn something useful from authors of the past, rather than to enjoy putting them down by means of a hyperliterate gamesmanship, is well illustrated by Derrida's mistreatment of Rousseau. Derrida's complaints against Rousseau, to put the matter as clearly as possible (which of course is ipso facto to misrepresent Derrida), seem to amount to the claim that he treats human nature both as a raw material on which education ought to be imposed and an ideal in relation to which both education and culture are characteristically defective. To any moderately intelligent reader who is disposed to find something helpful in Rousseau, the following possibility will soon occur. "Nature" as raw material in the human case includes certain potentialities These may either be fostered in such a way that a person is enabled and encouraged to achieve happiness and fulfilment in herself, and to promote happiness and fulfilment in others, or be frustrated in such a way as to lead to misery both in herself and in those unfortunate enough to come within the scope of her influence. Whatever one may think of Rousseau's conclusions, his basic questions are surely good, if one looks at them as posing the problem of how we can make the best out of our given (or "present") human potentialities. Are there perhaps, in the light of our overall conception of the human good, defects in conventional education, including a tendency to habituate people too much to luxurious habits and compulsions before they have the critical faculties to determine how far these are in the ultimate interests either of themselves or of their society at large? May Rousseau not be right in claiming that, in the light of this view of the good, it is bad if the child is taught to value means over ends, money or power over the pleasure or happiness to be gained by them?[45]

A similar point may be made about Derrida's attitude to Rousseau's concern with his sexuality and its objects. If a reader wants to make sense of Rousseau on this matter, she will soon come to see that he had at the back of his mind an ideal of sexual fulfilment (as one important aspect of the human good), such that persons might enjoy intense sexual delight without danger to their own or others' long-term well-being. At this rate, there is nothing to be wondered at in his judgment that, given the state of his health, masturbation was in some ways an option preferable to sexual intercourse, in spite of its palpable limitations; or that his foster-mother fulfilled his intimate needs in a manner that was in some ways superior to what was done by his mistress, though both fell short of what they might have been in this respect? (It would be instructive in this connection to have an account by Rousseau's mistress of how far *he* fulfilled

45. Cf. Marilyn French, *Beyond Power. On Women, Men and Morals* (New York: Summit Books, 1985).

her needs.) Is it not characteristic of a great many people, both female and male, that they hanker after an ideal of sexual fulfilment, which is implanted in them by nature or nurture or (most likely) a combination of the two, that they can never realize? This does not imply that they suffer from some mental confusion about a perfect "origin," in relation to which the "supplements" afforded by the course of life are in some contradictory way both necessary additions and debilitating corruptions. That the golden age supposed to have existed in the past, whether in the lives of individuals or the history of societies, is generally a compensatory projection of the frustrations of the present, is true and important. But it may be and has been far more clearly stated than is possible in terms of Derrida's terminology of "myth of origin," "presence," and "supplement."

In the case of the "hierarchical oppositions" described by Derrida, "one of two terms," he says, "governs the other. . . . To deconstruct the opposition . . . is to overturn the hierarchy at a given moment."[46] It is a fundamental concern of Derrida's thought that in such cases (to quote Boyne) one should "overturn the privilege of the high side and celebrate the secondary, derivative, low side: the supplement." In its reversing of polarities,and privileging of what was previously unprivileged, deconstruction seems at first sight to be clearly relevant to politics—the very essence of which is either to confirm hierarchy or to subvert it. It appears too that its lessons may be applied to injustices between the sexes, or between races and economic classes. We have Derrida's word for it that deconstruction intervenes, is not neutral.[47] But, as Boyne remarks, it is not at all clear what such intervention would amount to in concrete situations, or how it might be effective.[48]

46. Derrida, *Positions,* 41.
47. Ibid., 93.
48. Boyne, *Foucault,* 127, 129.

As a whole, Foucault's work indicates that power is inextricably bound up with social life as we know it. There seems a ray of hope for better things in *Madness and Civilization;* but scepticism had definitely taken over by the time that he wrote *Discipline and Punish.* In that work he shows modern subjects as totally involved as willing supports of the structures of capitalism, rather than as simply alienated or repressed by them. In *The History of Sexuality,* he provides yet further evidence of how far Western humanity has imprisoned itself; of how deeply the anti-difference mentality is ingrained in the Western mind, and of how great is the revolutionary effort that is needed to overcome it. And he thinks of power-relationships as dominating the very formation of our concepts and our views of truth. Such a perspective may well appear to issue in the conclusion that there is no prospect for a rational change of institutions, so political quietism would seem to be the only sensible response. Boyne concedes that this is a real problem and probably the reason why the work of both Foucault and Derrida is often criticized as essentially conservative. While their writings appear on the surface to be extremely radical, "neither has positive alternatives to offer against which the present system of knowledge or society can be measured." Unlike traditional intellectuals, they hold no illusions that they have "a place to stand in order to observe with any degree of detachment the society of which they form a part." They both applaud Marxism for exploding the claims of the bourgeoisie to know what is absolutely true and right, but condemn it for its confident prophecies of a society that will finally have done away with such illusions. Their only resort is to piecemeal and isolated criticism, which makes no appeal to what Jean-François Lyotard would call "metanarratives."[49]

49. Ibid., 124–25, 129–30, 132, 139.

While in general well-disposed to Foucault and Derrida, Roy Boyne admits that, if there are lessons in their work for feminism, anti-racism, or any other emancipatory social movement, they are not to be found on the surface. Indeed, he asks whether their "gloomy realism" leaves any basis for positive action, and he says that the question has no simple answer.[50] But in fact the answer is as plain as a pikestaff. On the principles—or rather anti-principles—which they both expound in the main body of their work, one either acts in a manner that is necessarily arbitrary, or one takes the easier way out of doing nothing. Thus Derrida's coyness about the actual effects which the adoption of his ideas would have on politics and university teaching should come as no surprise.[51] As to Foucault, it is hard not to agree with Nancy Fraser's view, that he oscillates between two inadequate attitudes—holding a conception of power that does not allow him to condemn any particular feature of modernity, while at the same time appearing to imply that modernity has nothing good about it. What he needs, as she says, are principles for distinguishing between appropriate and objectionable forms and uses of power.[52] Of the unfortunate implications of opposition without principle, one could scarcely find a more telling example than Foucault's remark, in a discussion dating from 1978, that an age barrier to sexual consent hardly makes sense, since children can be trusted to say whether or not they were subjected to coercion.[53] Here we seem to be faced, as Boyne well puts it, with "the kind of complacency that might be ex-

50. Ibid., 130, 136.

51. Cf. the quotation from "The Conflict of the Faculties" in Culler, *Deconstruction,* 156.

52. "Foucault on Modern Power: empirical insights and normative confusions," *Praxis International* (October 1981), 286; cited in Boyne, *Foucault,* 139–40.

53. *Politics, Philosophy and Culture,* ed. Lawrence D. Kritzman (London: Routledge, 1988), 284; cited in Boyne, *Foucault,* 140.

pected from someone who suspects everything and must therefore condemn nothing."[54]

According to the principles of the New Enlightenment, we have enough self-transcendence to attend to our present situation, to consider how it is and how it might be improved in the light of the idea of the good, and to plan and act accordingly. Foucault's recommendation, that a general political stance should be avoided, and that one should settle for particular political resistances and interventions instead, by no means solves the problem. This may easily be seen when one attends to the question of how any particular resistance or intervention might be justified. If no such justification can be given, all such actions are equally arbitrary; one might as well denounce or obstruct the relief of the poor, the liberation of the oppressed, or the emancipation of women, as speak or act on behalf of these good causes. But the only form that such justification can take is appeal to some general principle or other—like "It is wrong that some people should have hardly enough food or shelter to survive, while others live in luxury"; or "It is unfair that some human beings should be handicapped in their search for fulfilment and self-expression, merely on the grounds of their gender."

Indeed, no general criterion for the improvement of human life, at least as influenced by "Western rationality," turns out to be subtle enough to survive deconstructive analysis or Foucauldian pessimism. One is not surprised to read, for example, that neither Foucault nor Derrida would have any use for Herbert Marcuse's "romantic anti-capitalism."[55] But for all the crudities and oversimplifications that might be attributed to Marcuse, at least his work leads one to ponder an enormously important practical problem. How can we impose upon ourselves and others enough discipline for the maintenance and further develop-

54. Boyne, *Foucault,* 140.

55. Ibid., 128–29.

ment of science and technology, with all the obvious benefits which these confer upon us, without unduly spoiling the sweetness of spontaneous human life and emotional expression? Robin Horton has remarked on the zest in the immediate business of living which is so characteristic of members of "primitive" societies, in such sadly marked contrast to ourselves.[56] It is among the most attractive and plausible features of Marx's thought that, as technology and our understanding of human beings increases, we may look forward to an era when we may have the best of both worlds—or, at least, when we will have both the wisdom and the know how to find a far more satisfactory compromise than is enjoyed by the majority of people at present.[57] Cannot a sufficiently developed social science be expected to explain how, even if the dilemma cannot be resolved once and for all, its worst effects may at least be mitigated?

The fact is that, owing to the very nature of Foucault's and Derrida's thought in the main body of their work, any concrete suggestion about how human life might be improved must be sabotaged by their thought. Such a suggestion may be reasonable or unreasonable. If the former, they both pillory it as fatally compromised due to our corrupt Western philosophical dispositions; if the latter, why should anyone else take it seriously? The nettle has to be firmly grasped: either we have enough cognitive and moral self-transcendence to describe objectively and to criticize fundamental elements in our culture, or we do not. If we do not, quietism over important moral and political matters inevitably ensues. We have no moral or political Archimedean point, no firm critical base, from which to evaluate our society and culture, so we might just as well leave them alone.

56. Robin Horton, "African Traditional Thought and Western Science," in *Rationality,* ed. Bryan Wilson (Oxford: Blackwell, 1970), 170.

57. Cf. Hugo Meynell, *Freud, Marx and Morals* (Totowa, N.J.: Barnes and Noble, 1981), 85–86.

This is why Jürgen Habermas quite rightly castigates postmodernists for their "neoconservatism."

But someone might ask, how on earth could such transcendence of the contingencies of our historical situation be possible? The answer is simple. The thesis that haunts postmodernism—that reality as it is and has been prior to and independently of human society might be impossible to grasp by means of our concepts and judgments—is at bottom incoherent, since we can form no coherent idea of the real apart from that to which our concepts and judgments refer so far as we are as rational as possible. From within our social situations, we can get to know about things and states of affairs (thermonuclear processes in the sun, continental drift, the anatomy of Triceratops) which existed prior to and independently of our social situation. By the same token, we may envisage possibilities of justice and happiness among human beings which are not now realized in our societies, and perhaps have never been realized, but may yet be used as yardsticks by means of which the quality of our lives may be measured. The special flavor of much postmodernist writing is due to the fact that the possibility of such moral self-transcendence, without which no fundamental criticism of one's society or culture is possible, is at once implicitly taken for granted and explicitly denied. The detection and correction of such "performative self-contradictions" is, as we have seen, close to the heart of the New Enlightenment.

Modern Western society appears to provide us with a great many benefits and conveniences at the cost of some irksome restrictions and disciplines. The New Enlightenment is inclined to press the very practical general question of how, people being as they are or might be, we can at once maximize the benefits and minimize the restrictions. Postmodernism seems to be committed to a curious oscillation between a violent moral hectoring—which one would have thought could be justified only on the basis of objective norms of good and bad, right and wrong—

and a total normlessness, which makes nonsense of any moral stance whatever. It is a tribute to Foucault, however, that he seems to realize by instinct that the problems of society in general are nicely caught in microcosm by those of the administration of mental hospitals and prisons. How, in each case, can one have enough supervision and restraint to prevent people from harming others and themselves, at the same time permitting enough privacy and self-direction for them to lead some semblance of a human life?

In Foucault's latest works, there is a more positive direction indicated for moral and social reform. Discipline now seems to have a place, but, in Boyne's words, "this time it is not so much a question of an alienating imposition, rather one of normatively reinforced self-regulation." In *A History of Sexuality,* Foucault commends an ancient Greek ideal: as he sees it, while modern persons, scarred by the long history of Christianity, are made or rather marred by imposed authority, the Greeks may be said to have formed themselves as moral subjects over the course of their lives. One might indeed put it that, for Foucault in his latest writings, the root of the evils that beset modern society is that we are not Greek enough. Christian purity has set an impossible standard, which has led inevitably to a deep rift between theory and practice. So far as the Greek was concerned, persons were expected to mold their own characters in the direction of ideals that were at least in principle achievable, rather than merely to weep with loathing over their actual or supposed shortcomings.[58] For the Greek, Foucault says, "more important than the content of the law and its conditions of application was the attitude that caused one to respect them. The accent was placed on the relationship with the self that enabled a person to keep from being carried away by the appetites and pleasures, to

58. Boyne, *Foucault,* 144, 147, 149.

maintain a mastery and superiority over them, to keep his senses in a state of tranquillity, to remain free from interior bondage to the passions, and to achieve a mode of being that could be defined by the full enjoyment of oneself, or the perfect supremacy of oneself over oneself."[59] The ideal appears to have been a permanent effort at self-formation, in accordance with what Foucault calls "an aesthetics of existence." The training involved was supposed to be not only of benefit to the individual, but a prerequisite for the conduct of civil affairs or the running of a household.[60] "The freedom of individuals, understood as the mastery they were capable of exercising over themselves, was indispensable to the entire state. . . . The individual's attitude towards himself, the way in which he ensured his own freedom with regard to himself, and the form of supremacy he maintained over himself were a contributary element to the well-being and good order of the city."[61] Unfortunately, he says, things are quite different in our own time, where the exercise of power without responsibility seems to be the rule rather than the exception.[62]

It is to be noted that a kind of knowledge (presumably that of one's own capacities and limitations) was a necessary condition of such moderation and self-discipline; to make oneself the ideal person in the Greek sense thus included the acquisition of this kind of knowledge. This is as much as to say that "the logos be placed in a position of supremacy in the human being and that it be able to subdue the desires and regulate behaviour."[63] Greek women, unfortunately, were not supposed to be able to represent this ideal, due to a passivity imposed on them by society. The Greeks in general took male superiority to be

59. Foucault, *The Use of Pleasure* (Harmondsworth: Penguin Books, 1986), 31.

60. Ibid., 75–76.

61. Ibid., 79.

62. Cf. Boyne, *Foucault*, 144–49.

63. Foucault, *Use*, 86.

"natural." But as Derrida shows in his discussion of Rousseau, this kind of justification is merely ideological. It would seem to be a consequence of these later views of Foucault that revolutionaries and social reformers ought to decry and resist those kinds of exercise of power that are not tempered by self-mastery or care for others.[64]

A similar positive direction may be seen in the later writings of Derrida, particularly in relation to *apartheid* and the case of Paul de Man. Derrida's usual preoccupation with affirming difference seems at odds with some remarks of his about racial inequality, where he commits himself in effect to the reality of an objective moral law and conception of duty, however vestigial these may be, and however rarely it is proper to evoke them. He writes of oppositions that are beyond deconstruction when he affirms unequivocally the moral superiority of the cause of the Blacks to that of the Whites in South Africa. (It should be noted that this was before the abolition of apartheid.) For Derrida, Nelson Mandela has been admirable for his devotion to a principle that is above any law that can be enacted by a state, that is, the innate equality of all human beings. "He presents himself in his people, before the law. Before a law he rejects, beyond any doubt, but which he rejects in the name of a superior law, the very one he declares to admire and before which he agrees to appear."[65] On Derrida's view, the equality of human beings, without respect to their race, is inscribed in Western thought but flouted by the action of Westerners; here at least it is inappropriate to deconstruct Western reason as such. He strongly confirms what he takes to be Mandela's view, "that to be Black" (to put it in Boyne's words) "is not to be essentially

64. Boyne, *Foucault,* 149, 151.

65. "The Laws of Reflection: Nelson Mandela, in Admiration," in J. Derrida and Mustapha Tilli, eds., *For Nelson Mandela* (New York: Seaver, 1987), 15.

different; but that Black is forced to be different, and that Black would wish the freedom to be the same; and that freedom would be the opening of the road to non-coercive (in either direction) difference." Not only does Derrida praise Mandela's invitation to share the dream of Western reason; he cites Mandela's description of the "origin" which Westerners have perverted. "There were no classes, no rich or poor, and no exploitation of man by man. . . . In such a society are contained the seeds of a revolutionary democracy in which poverty, want and insecurity shall be no more."[66]

In 1988, Derrida published a long article on the revelations that had recently emerged about the activities of Paul de Man during the Second World War.[67] Derrida admitted that it was quite inexcusable of de Man, to publish over a hundred articles in a pro-Nazi newsapaper in German-occupied Belgium. It may be conceded that, even in 1942 when he wrote the last article, de Man knew nothing of Auschwitz. But he did know that Jews had been forced to sell businesses, had been herded into special cities, and were being beaten up on the streets. The central point of Derrida's lengthy and complex response, as Boyne sees it, was that "de Man did something unacceptable but then entirely broke with it, and spent the rest of his working and writing life constructing a testament against his past."[68]

In the later writings of Foucault and Derrida, it looks as though at last common sense and common decency proved too strong for principle. Foucault came to see that a discipline that was such as to harmonize and coordinate the passions was worth cultivating, and that the ideal of self-mastery with a view to

66. Derrida and Tilli, *Mandela,* 24.

67. "Like the sound of the sea deep within a shell: Paul de Man's war" *Critical Inquiry* 14 (Spring 1988), 590–652.

68. Boyne's italics. Boyne, *Foucault,* 158–59.

social responsibility could be used as a basis for criticism of many of our own practices and the beliefs that support them. Derrida decided that the "hierarchical opposition" between good and bad, between what a decent person should implement or defend and what she should not, was not ripe for "deconstruction" in the case of the cause of the Blacks in South Africa. To put Derrida's pronouncements on the matter with very un-Derridean crudity and directness, the cause of the Blacks was *good,* while the cause of the Whites who oppressed them was *bad.* Boyne will have it that these developments amount to "a reaffirmation, all the stronger for having been tested, of that law above the law."[69] It amounts to no such thing; it is a complete *volte face,* quite incompatible with the clear implications of earlier remarks by these authors. Furthermore, while the moral and political viewpoint toward which Foucault appears ultimately to have been reaching is certainly commendable, it is quite unoriginal. It is a blend (as I believe all sane moral philosophy must be) of the principles of Aristotle and Kant, and corresponds closely to one strand of traditional Christian ethics, that represented most notably by Thomas Aquinas, with his maxim that grace does not take away nature, but perfects it. The ideal is a free yet ordered self-development and self-expression, which is disciplined in the interest of its own long-term ends and those of others. In other words, it is the ideal of the New Enlightenment, to which deconstruction and anti-rationalism contribute little but conceptual confusion and practical hindrance. As to "democracy," it is misleading to conceive of it as any kind of "origin," since, in the form envisaged by Mandela and commended by Derrida, it has never yet existed. It is rather an ideal, to which actual social and political arrangements ought to approximate, and for falling far short of which they ought to be criticized.

69. Ibid., 158.

Derrida's discussion of de Man makes the sensible point that the merit of a person's moral or political attitudes at one stage of her career is not necessarily vitiated by what she has done or written at another stage. But it is surely a great deal too much to say that the later writings of de Man amount to anything approaching a repudiation of the attitudes evinced in his earlier work. On the contrary, one has the unpleasant feeling that the moral nihilism which seems to be insinuated through the notorious obscurities of de Man's later writings, is no less amenable to Nazi propaganda than it is to any other moral or immoral stance. It may be conceded that de Man was strongly opposed to the aestheticism of Heidegger, and that Heidegger was himself for many years associated with Nazism. But one can appreciate Heidegger's splendid corrective to modern obsession with technology and control without going on to romanticize any kind of political brutality.[70] Certainly there is a danger in bringing the same kind of palpitating receptivity to a political party or program as to forested landscape or a painting by van Gogh. But a thoroughgoing application of New Enlightenment rationality can easily determine where such attitudes are appropriate, where inappropriate, and why.

Among those said to have been influenced by Derrida, Abdul Jan Mohamed is surely right that economic requirements have led to racial stereotypes.[71] If black persons were needed as drudges, it was convenient to justify their being such by claiming or assuming that they were "naturally" inferior, savage, stupid, and so on. But, for reasons that I have already stressed at length, it is more useful to see such phenomena as a matter of the "flight from insight" identified by the New Enlightenment than in terms of "binary oppositions" to be "deconstructed." Much the same is to be said about Edward Said's aspersions on

70. See Hugo Meynell, *Redirecting*, chap. 9.
71. Boyne, *Foucault*, 157.

anthropology, which he claims is shot throughwith the influence of binary oppositions reflecting White bias.[72] No doubt the categories used by anthropologists are greatly affected by Foucault's "power/knowledge complex," but so are those of every form of inquiry, from physics through palaeontology to literary history The problems, however, are undoubtedly more acute in the human sciences, where the temptation of the scholar to justify her own prejudices at the expense of her subject of study is especially severe. Said will have it that it is useful to have identified what is wrong, even if at present it is impossible to see how the error can be rectified. But it is not in the least difficult to specify in general terms, from the point of view of the New Enlightenment, how mistakes of this kind can be put right. In anthropology, just as in the case of other subjects, one has to determine how far conclusions have been sought for and established with a thoroughgoing rationality, rather than in accordance with the bias that favors the interest of the individual inquirer, her immediate associates, her paymasters, or her social or racial group.

72. Ibid., 158.

4

POSTMODERNISM II

LYOTARD AND RORTY

ACCORDING to Jean-François Lyotard, knowledge consists not only of the ability to make "good" descriptive statements—about how things are in the world (that Toulouse is the name of a town in France, that a beryllium atom contains four protons, and so on)—but also "good" prescriptive and evaluative ones—about how things ought to be and what one is to do. What makes all of them "good" is conformity with the standards of truth, justice, efficiency, beauty, and so on, that prevail within the society concerned. It also includes what is called "knowhow"—as when one says that someone knows how to live, to listen, or to conduct themselves at a public auction. Now scientific knowledge exists, and has done so from the first, alongside and more or less in conflict with what may be called "narrative knowledge," which is a matter of custom and transmits the rules that hold a society together. For scientific knowledge, denotation is the only object, and all other language-games are excluded. To be a scientist is to be able to make statements about entities that are accessible to experts, and for the statements to be verifiable or falsifiable. These characteristics are what distinguish science from the language-games constitutive of the social bonds that make up narrative knowledge. It is pointless to evaluate scientific knowledge on the basis of narrative knowledge, or narrative on the basis of scientific; the criteria for the two sorts of knowledge are completely different from one another.[1]

Narrative knowledge is not bothered with questions of its own legitimation, and makes little appeal to argument or proof. It is apt to approach science in a tolerant spirit, as just one more kind of narrative. However, the converse by no means holds. On the ground that narrative statements are not subject to argument or proof, scientists are prone to dismiss them as "savage, primitive, undeveloped, backward, alienated, composed of opinions, customs, authority, prejudice, ignorance, ideology. Narratives are fables, myths, legends, fit only for women and children."[2] However, it is to be noted that scientists themselves, when they seek to justify their calling in the newspapers or on television, adopt the procedures of narrative knowledge and present an account of science as a kind of epic. In this they are supported by the State, whose decision makers need the same epic to bolster their own credibility. Such a resort to narrative knowledge is only to be expected, since a moment's reflection will show that attempts to legitimate science cannot themselves form a part of science.[3] "Scientific knowledge cannot know or make known that it is the true knowledge without resorting to the other, narrative, kind of knowledge which from its point of view is no knowledge at all. Without such recourse it would be in the position of presupposing its own validity and would be stooping to what it condemns: begging the question. But does it not fall into the same trap by using narrative as its authority?"[4]

1. J.-F. Lyotard, *The Postmodern Condition* (Minneapolis: University of Minnesota Press, 1984), 7, 18–19, 21, 25–26.

2. Ibid., 27.

3. Ibid., 27–28.

4. Ibid., 29.

Science has posed the problem of its own legitimation throughout its history, as can be seen clearly from the work of Plato. The famous allegory of the cave in his *Republic,* a piece of narrative if ever there was one, illustrates Lyotard's point very well. It is part of an attempt to vindicate the scientific attitude, and associates this, most instructively from Lyotard's point of view, with the problem of social and political authority. (Within the cave, one sees merely distorted reflections of things. Only one who has ventured outside knows how things really are, and will have a tough job to put this over to those who have always remained inside.)[5] Descartes' case is very similar, since, in the *Discourse on Method,* he justifies scientific method in terms of a narrative about his own mental processes. With the rise of science in its strictly modern sense, the quest for metaphysical foundations is left behind, and it is assumed that nothing but the consensus of experts is required to validate the rules that are followed. However, narrative knowledge made a come back in the social and political sphere, when the bourgeoisie began to assert themselves against their former masters. A new hero was set up: the people. But they soon proceeded to ape the methods of the scientists. Thus they still "debate among themselves about what is just or unjust in the same way that the scientific community debates about what is true or false; they accumulate civil laws just as scientists accumulate scientific laws; they perfect their rules of consensus just as scientists produce new 'paradigms.'"[6] Such procedures are quite different from those associated with traditional narrative knowledge, which makes no pretense to either universality or to cumulative advance. And as the new political and social wisdom imitates the methods and

5. F. M. Cornford suggested that the cinema would have been a better analogy. See *Plato. The Republic,* trans. H. D. P. Lee (Harmondsworth: Penguin Books, 1955), 278.

6. Lyotard, *Postmodern,* 30.

attitudes of science, it is no wonder that it too should set itself to destroy the traditional narrative knowledges of various cultures, on the ground that they are nothing but a farrago of ignorance and obscurantism.[7]

According to Lyotard, what the Sophists of Plato's time have to teach us is that there is no knowledge in ethics or politics, only opinion.[8] Prescriptions cannot be reduced to descriptions, even to descriptions taken in Platonic fashion from a superior realm. The assumption that knowledge is available in these areas is bound to lead to "rationalist terrorism," whether in the name of capitalism, communism, or even of progressive human liberation. Lyotard endorses the Sophists' questioning of conventions and unsettling of received opinions. However, he would by no means agree with their alleged objective of getting people to think and do whatever the Sophist wanted. It is characteristic of rationalist terrorism to attack root and branch any claim, policy, or institution that cannot be justified in a scientific or quasi-scientific manner. In fact it is the demand for legitimation that is at the root of the cultural imperialism that has dogged Western civilization since its beginnings. The real issue in modernity is an insatiable and inexorable will-to-power imposing itself by way of rational calculation.[9] The horrifying events of the twentieth century, of which the bombing of Hiroshima and the camp at Auschwitz are outstanding examples, have utterly discredited the project of modernism so far as Lyotard is concerned. He says that postmodernity is inaugurated by the new crime of "populocide."[10] As against the dismal and destructive

7. Ibid., 28–30.

8. The contradiction between this claim and the one we have just attributed to Lyotard is only superficial. In the earlier context, Lyotard is including under the rubric of "narrative knowledge" what he here distinguishes from "knowledge as opinion."

9. Lyotard, "Rules and Paradoxes and Svelte Appendix," *Cultural Critique* 5 (1986), 216.

10. *Le Postmoderne expliqué aux enfants* (Paris: Galilee, 1986), 40.

consistency of the modern, the principle of postmodern knowledge "is not the expert's homology, but the inventors paralogy."[11] A propos of some of his own work, Lyotard protests that it is by no means intended to *argue for* anything. Of one of his own books, he says that its writing "perpetrates a kind of violence. . . . What is scandalous about it is that it is all rhetoric. . . . This kind of writing is generally taken to be that of the rhetorician and persuader, that is . . . of the sly one, the one who deceives. To me, it is the opposite. . . . It presupposes that the reader does not allow himself or herself to be dominated."[12]

Lyotard makes a great deal of that notion of "language-games" which was put into philosophical currency by Ludwig Wittgenstein in his *Philosophical Investigations.*[13] No unified "story," as Lyotard sees it, is to be found, and no foundation is to be reached. Language-games are simply irreducible to one another, and none is to be justified in terms of anything else. In ideal circumstances, we would be as frequently as possible inventing new language-games, and new moves in old ones. But it must always be remembered that, however various language-games may be, they cannot represent what constantly reaches beyond them—desire and life. Competition between language-games is to be settled by something more like aesthetic judgment than rationality. As David Kolb puts it, for Lyotard "(a) new language-game may sweep us along or answer to desires that go beyond their present articulation." In effect, a society is to be commended, on Lyotard's account, to the degree that it tolerates a wide variety of language-games. Such an ideal, of course, is far removed indeed from life today, afflicted as it is by the paralysis of bureaucracy.[14] Lyotard tries to insist on justice

11. Lyotard, *Postmodern,* xxv.

12. Lyotard, *Just Gaming,* 4–5. David Kolb, *Postmodern Sophistications* (Chicago and London: University of Chicago Press, 1990), 36, 37, 43, 48, 83.

13. Oxford: Blackwell, 1958.

14. Lyotard, *Postmodern,* 17.

between players of different language-games, without appealing to any higher game to the rules of which they are all bound to conform.[15]

We should contemplate a wide variety of types and uses of language with delight, "just as we do . . . the diversity of plant or animal species."[16] Still, it will not do to overlook the element of competition between them. "To speak is to fight . . . speech-acts fall within the domain of a general agonistics. . . . Great joy is had in the endless invention of turns of phrase, of words and meanings. . . . But undoubtedly even this pleasure depends on a feeling of success won at the expense of an adversary." It should be added, however, that the adversary may not be personal, but only the generally accepted set of conventions governing language at any given place and time.[17] "One writes against language, but necessarily with it. To say what it already knows how to say is not writing. One wants to say what it does not know how to say. . . . One violates it, one seduces it, one introduces into it an idiom which it had not known. But when that same desire to be able to say something other than what has been already said—has disappeared, and language is experienced as impenetrable and inert rendering vain all writing, then it is called Newspeak."[18]

There are many heterogeneous language-games whose users make up society. Those who hold power assume that these language-games are all commensurable. Efficient performance, in their eyes, is what legitimates every position either on truth or on social justice. The application of this criterion to all language-games again results in a kind of terrorism—"be operational, or disappear."[19] The sort of expert that is favored by

15. Kolb, *Sophistications,* 36–38, 46–47, 49.

16. Lyotard, *Postmodern,* 27.

17. Ibid., 10.

18. Lyotard, *Enfants;* cited in J. Pefanis, *Heterology and the Postmodern* (Durham, N.C., and London: Duke University Press, 1991), 83.

19. Lyotard, *Postmodern,* xxiv.

establishments "knows what he knows and what he does not know," whereas the philosopher, as typified by Lyotard himself, does not. "One concludes, the other questions—two very different language-games."[20]

It is characteristic of Lyotard to proclaim that what he calls "metanarratives" have reached a crisis. Most narratives turn out to be fables when judged in the light of science. However, when science itself aspires to search for the truth, as opposed to merely pointing out regularities that happen to be useful, it is compelled to seek legitimation for itself. This it does by appealing to what is called philosophy. One may designate as "modern" any science that tries to legitimate itself in this way, appealing to one or other of such "grand narrative(s)" as "the dialectics of Spirit, the hermeneutics of meaning, the emancipation of the rational or working subject, or the creation of wealth."[21] Greatly to oversimplify, one might say that postmodernism is a matter of "incredulity toward metanarratives."[22] The Enlightenment metanarrative was cast in terms of a hoped-for agreement between reasonable minds, and the universal peace that it was believed would result from this. The question is often raised of where legitimacy can reside, after the demise of metanarratives. At least technological efficiency is not a relevant criterion for truth or justice. The trouble with the criterion advocated by Jürgen Habermas—consensus achieved by dint of rational discussion—is that it does violence to the variety and multiplicity of actual and possible language-games, and in addition it neglects the fact that dissension is the very womb of invention.[23]

Unexpectedly enough, Lyotard rejects the relativism and conventionalism about value that is supposed to have been characteristic of the Sophists. He thinks that acceptance of such a position would lead to what is called "consensus" politics, where

20. Ibid., xxv.
21. Ibid., xxiii.
22. Ibid., xxiv.
23. Ibid., xxiii–xxv.

whatever a group agrees upon is "right for" them. "But we know what that means: the manufacture of a subject that is authorized to say 'we.' "[24] Such a politics would inevitably give rise to injustices, which we must oppose even though we can assign no well-grounded reasons for doing so. However, given that conflicts are inevitable, and given that there is no universal mode of thinking or speaking by which to regulate them, how are we to avoid such conclusions as "might makes right"? In *Le Differend,*[25] Lyotard suggests that one can appeal to something akin to what Kant calls an "Idea." (An Idea in this sense is, as David Kolb puts it, "an extension of an existing concept into a description of an unrealized state, a goal that may be impossible to experience [or even contradictory were it to be realized] but can still guide our judgment by giving it a direction. The irreducible differences between the various kinds of language games can be so extended into an Idea.")[26] There is to be none of the modernist searching for more and more adequate grounds. Rather, we should constantly be looking for new games, and new rules in old ones. A new way of painting, or a new way of managing a commercial enterprise, might presuppose an implicit criticism of what went before as insufficiently capable of fulfilling our desires. But there is no question of progress toward any ideal way of living. Further, it is an inescapable fact that there are claims placed upon us by others to which we have to listen, and yet there is no rule to inform us beforehand of the nature of these claims or how we ought to meet them. Some prescriptions that might be thought to issue from the claims made on us by others are unjust; none can be taken as definitive. As Kolb expresses Lyotard's position on the matter, "We are addressed;

24. Lyotard, *Just Gaming,* 81.

25. Lyotard, *The Differend: Phrases in Dispute* (Minneapolis: University of Minnesota Press, 1988).

26. Kolb, *Sophistications,* 38.

we are called to respond; but we must judge how to respond in each particular case. In doing so, we have no rules to follow."[27]

As Habermas sees it, Lyotard's views do not leave open the possibility of genuine criticism of our practices and goals. Habermas himself, though, does not believe that any absolute foundation, in the Platonic sense, can be provided for such criticism. On his account it is enough for rational agents, if they are to coordinate their actions, to be able and willing to meet one another's challenges about the truth of what they say, their sincerity in saying it, and its appropriateness to the circumstances. The results achieved by such interaction admittedly can never be anything but provisional, as its principles are irreducibly procedural in nature. Lyotard pillories Habermas for his pains as "a dinosaur of the Enlightenment."[28] As for Habermas's concern with consensus, Lyotard writes: "(T)he problem is not consensus . . . but the unpresentable, the unexpected power of the Idea, the event as the presentation of an unknown and unacceptable phrase which then gains acceptance by force of experience."[29]

Lyotard and Habermas are, however, at one in being concerned about the way in which the mass media level out differences. They also both deplore the tendency in education to concentrate on technical efficiency at the expense of inventiveness and the capacity to communicate. They want power and voice to be conferred on suppressed and marginalized groups. Both are concerned with justice, though this is largely a matter of consensus for Habermas, and for Lyotard of emphasizing while respecting differences.[30] Some have ventured to wonder whether Lyotard is not a liberal at heart, for all the radical atti-

27. Ibid., 39, 37.

28. Lyotard, "Judicieux dans le differend," in *La Faculté de Juger* (Paris: Editions de Minuit, 1985), 168.

29. Lyotard, "Rules"; cf. *Postmodern,* 81–82. Kolb, *Sophistications,* 39–41.

30. Kolb, *Sophistications,* 45–46.

tudes that he strikes. But he himself vehemently repudiates the imputation. "Does what I say lead to an advocacy of neoliberalism? Not in the least. Neoliberalism is itself an illusion. The reality is concentration in industrial, social, and financial empires served by the States and political classes."[31]

Lyotard is right to point out that we speak of "knowing how" as well as "knowing that"; but I do not think that the point is really relevant to the problem to which he applies it—that of how scientific "knowledge that" is related to "knowledge that" of other kinds. In general, as I have remarked already, Plato's suggestion in the *Theaetetus* seems to be on the right lines, that knowledge is true belief supported by appropriate justification. When someone has believed something, for however good reason, and it turns out not to be so, we will generally deny that she knew it. And when someone makes a lucky guess out of the blue, for no assignable reason, which turns out to be correct, we may well say, "Well, she had good luck in her guessing; but she didn't really *know* it." These points seem to apply both to scientific knowledge and opinion and to knowledge and opinion of other kinds. I have claimed, following the epistemology of the New Enlightenment, that beliefs are justified so far as they are rationally (attentively, intelligently, and reasonably) arrived at or maintained, and that beliefs tend to converge on truth so far as they are so justified. We accept the authority of scientists within their specialties, and are right to do so, on the assumption that they or their informants have had opportunity to come up with the most rational available beliefs about the matters with which they deal.

Lyotard accuses both science and popular democracy of an arrogant and destructive approach to tradition and established custom—I regard his locution "narrative knowledge" as very

31. Lyotard, "Rules," 218.

misleading, for reasons that will appear. Now if one is concerned with truth or with the good, traditions and established customs would seem at first sight to be rather a mixed bag. More attention to the matter surely confirms this initial impression. Such established customs as strangling people to death out of devotion to a goddess, or throwing live widows on the funeral pyres of their dead husbands, or binding the feet of girl children to prevent their growth, seem to me rather bad, however hallowed they are by tradition—and the reason is simply that they are unfair and cause a great deal more misery than happiness. (There may have seemed to be good reason for burning people alive when it was thought to prevent their souls from being damned for eternity, but I think it would generally be agreed that our ancestors were quite sensible in discontinuing the practice when they came to doubt whether it was very effective for the purpose.)

On the other hand, some traditions and customs turn out, when subjected to rational investigation, to be harmless, others to be positively beneficial; others still seem to have both benefits and disadvantages. It appears to be a good idea, all things considered, that daggers and sheath knives should not be permitted in schools where violence among students is a problem. On the other hand, the *kirpan* is a symbol of great significance for the Sikh religion, which itself has many worthwhile features, including that it provides the meaning of life for some millions of people whose contribution to the public good seems if anything rather above the average. Perhaps some compromise is possible in this case (for example, model *kirpans* made out of some harmless material to be worn by children in schools); or else the lesser value, whichever it is deemed to be after extensive rational consideration of the relevant facts, should give way to the greater. Lyotard is probably correct in maintaining that one incidental effect of the Old Enlightenent has been an unwarranted contempt for tradition and established custom as such. But he is surely wrong to go to the opposite extreme, of in effect recommending a free-for-all. One of the main consequences of the New Enlightenment, it seems to me, is a thorough scrutiny of traditions and established customs, to see how far they are based on assumptions that are true, and how far on ones that are erroneous, and how far they are bad, or harmless, or good, or partly bad and partly good, and whether they should be retained, modified or abandoned accordingly. For example, one might ask how far the association of a woman and a man together in order to found a family tends to be stabilized by the taking of public vows and a social gathering; or whether segregation in boarding schools apart from the opposite sex has a beneficial long-term effect on the characters of boys and girls. As Lyotard implies, it is not very usual for those who cleave to traditions and established customs to attend much to the problem of their legitimation. But this by no means implies that it is not the right, or even the duty, of enlightened and conscientious persons to attend to the matter.

Just as the present conclusions of science have to be constantly and rigorously evaluated with a view to what is true, so customs, traditions, and social arrangements should be scrutinized with a view to what is good, and also in regard to the question of whether the assumptions on which they are based are true or false. (A custom based on a false assumption will rarely be beneficial, just as a moon-shot based on a thoroughly faulty theory of gravitation is unlikely to be successful.) As to "narratives," at least in the ordinary sense of the term, one may ask whether they are myth, legend, or history, or a mixture of some or all of these, and what legitimating, commendatory, or repressive function they may have. A medieval European story about a gang of cruel and mendacious Jews abducting and killing a Christian child is likely to have been an invention, given that many people were motivated to tell such tales. It also offered pretexts to many people to indulge their most vicious instincts by persecuting a conveniently identifiable alien group.

It is said of the Greek Cypriot leader General Grivas that he recommended the invention of atrocity stories about the British colonial administration, in order that resistance to it should be more determined and passionate. At the other extreme, there is the story of the king of Denmark, when his country was in the power of the Nazis, riding out with a Star of David on his arm on the day when all Jews had been ordered to wear this emblem. This story, though I understand (to my regret) that it is false, was evidently concocted and told for very different reasons and to very different effect than the story mentioned before it. Tales of these kinds, as Lyotard hints by his rather broad use of the notion of "narrative," can have a very important effect in maintaining or subverting desirable or undesirable patterns of behavior. But he is utterly wrong to claim that it is pointless or even harmful to scrutinize them on general principles in the light of what is likely to be true, or to conduce most to people's long-term good.

I have already argued at some length that, on New Enlightenment principles, the methods of science can be vindicated as liable to yield the truth about the matters with which they deal. Briefly, one can argue that (1) to be rational in the sense that I have given is in general the most reliable way of finding out the truth about things; and that (2) the mature physical sciences have applied these principles in a thoroughgoing way to a wide range of phenomena. It may be said that these two propositions themselves are in one sense scientific, in another sense not. As based upon comprehensively rational principles, they are so; but they form no part of any mature and established natural or social science. Let us call such propositions, and the arguments supposed to establish them, "transcendental." The claim of scientific method to lead us to the truth about things can be established by transcendental arguments. Lyotard presents his readers with a dilemma: either science purports to establish its own claim to truth, which it can only do by begging the question; or it must appeal to "narrative" justifications of a kind that on its own premisses are to be dismissed as unsatisfactory. The dilemma may be rebutted as follows. The claims of science to approach the truth in the matters with which it deals can be vindicated by transcendental arguments, which, as I have just said, may in a sense may be regarded as "scientific"; they are certainly not a matter of "narrative knowledge" in Lyotard's sense, given that such "knowledge" neither requires justification nor may usefully seek for it. How far the arguments of Plato or Descartes effectively ground science is moot. But whether they do so or not, it is important to recognize that, as Lyotard and other postmodernists would admit, this is what they were trying to do. And a sharp distinction should be made between their arguments as such on the one hand, and on the other the parables, stories, autobiographical anecdotes, and so on, which they used as literary devices to put their arguments across more effectively to their readers. Lyotard presents his case as though Plato's parable of the cave, and Descartes' reminiscence about himself and the stove, were crucial for these philosophers' arguments as such. But they are not. Furthermore, even if their arguments do not as such succeed, Plato and Descartes were adumbrating the successful resolution, in the epistemology of the New Enlightenment, of the problems about the legitimation of science with which they were concerned. The "narrative" justifications by scientists of their work on the media may be accounted for in the same way, though it may be doubted whether the education of most scientists would enable them to expound the real, transcendental justification for their work, even given the ability of a popular audience to appreciate it. It is worth adding that lack of apparent philosophical justification for the scientist's work in terms of the Old Enlightenment has encouraged postmodernism as a reaction and shows the importance of adopting New Enlightenment principles—granted that one values science—as providing such justification.[32]

The New Enlightenment follows the course that Lyotard (I think rightly) ascribes to Aristotle, of "separating the rules to which statements declared scientific must conform (the *Organon*) from the search for their legitimacy in a discourse on Being (the *Metaphysics*)."[33] That one is apt to arrive at the truth about the world by a certain method implies that the world must have a corresponding nature and structure. As Lonergan wrote, "Thoroughly understand what it is to understand, and you will understand the broad lines of all there is to be understood."[34] Lyotard is also right, I believe, in linking the problem of the justification of science with that of the justification of social authority in general. The authority of scientists is to be encouraged *because* and *insofar as* they carry out procedures liable to lead to discovery of the truth about things. That of our political and social superiors is to be encouraged insofar as they carry out procedures liable to establish and maintain the good of society. Representative democracy is to be commended because, for all its notorious liability to error and abuse, it seems less unlikely to realize the good and avoid the bad than any other known political system. As Churchill said, democracy is a rotten way of government, but it is better than all known alternatives.

Lyotard's view, that soundly based "knowledge" as opposed to mere "opinion" (in the senses corresponding to Plato's *episteme* and *doxa*) is impossible in the realms of morality and politics, is a typical symptom of ideological disappointment: some claimants to such knowledge let you down, so you never trust

32. The scandal of the lack of articulated justification for science preoccupied Edmund Husserl throughout his career.

33. Lyotard, *Postmodern,* 29.

34. *Insight,* "Introduction" and "Epilogue" (22 and 769 of the second edition).

another. Lyotard believes—and here I would largely agree with him—that two influential ideological products of the Old Enlightenment, Marxism and Freudianism, have largely failed to deliver on their promises.[35] He infers from this that no form of the Platonic quest for an ethics and politics that are rational—that is to say, founded securely on reasons rather than consisting of unjustified and unjustifiable opinions—is really possible. But at that rate there would be no reliable basis for any judgment of comparative value in assessing human actions or institutions, and this is palpably absurd. There are no doubt some defects in the present Liberal government of Canada presided over by Jean Chretien. But can we not really judge with good reason that it is better than the government of England under Stephen and Matilda, or of Mongolia under Genghis Khan? When it comes to the more private sphere of ethics, is the belief not well founded, that giving succor to the deprived and outcast is better than spouse-beating or the sexual exploitation of children? Nor are the reasons that underly these beliefs in doubt, for all that we seldom have occasion to make them explicit. The policy of Jean Chretien's government, and the practice of helping the deprived and outcast, tend on the whole to increase the sum of human happiness and fulfilment consistently with fairness; governments like Genghis Khan's and practices like child abuse, besides being very unfair on some people, increase the general sum of human frustration and misery. We have clear overall criteria for the moral, political, and social good, in other words; and these can be and ought to be rationally applied to the critique of human actions and institutions, just as the overall criteria of truth are and ought to be applied in science.

Whatever the incidental defects of the Old Enlightenment, Lyotard's claim—that its ideals led to the horrors of Auschwitz

35. On Lyotard's disappointment with Freud and Marx, see Pefanis, *Heterology,* 89. The title of his collection of 1973 (*Derivé à partir de Marx et Freud* ["Adrift from Marx and Freud"] [Paris: 10/18 UGE]) is symptomatic.

and Hiroshima—is grossly unfair. And it should be noted that, if one takes seriously the general opposition to cognitive and evaluative norms affected by Lyotard and other postmodernists, no imputation of moral evil would be defensible, since such defense could hardly amount to anything other than the giving of reasons. Certainly, the science and technology that are one legacy of the Old Enlightenment had their part to play in these horrors, especially in the case of the bomb that destroyed Hiroshima. But the main cause of the setting-up of camps like Auschwitz was a view of the nature and implications of racial and other differences that went totally against the intellectual thrust of the Old Enlightenment, to say nothing of its moral ideals. The Hiroshima case, though one has a great deal of compunction about saying so, has in any case more moral ambiguity about it than that of Auschwitz. It could be, and indeed has been, argued, that had the bomb not been dropped, even more suffering and loss of life would very probably have ensued. Certainly, such phenomena as Auschwitz and the events leading up to Hiroshima show a serious limitation in the Old Enlightenment; the dark human passions are not so easily set aside as was supposed by some of its more confident advocates.[36]

As for the "expert's homology" and the "inventor's paralogy," supposed by Lyotard to typify modernity and postmodernism respectively, the New Enlightenment has a use for both. The latter is needed at the level of intelligence, where the envisagement of fresh hypotheses is in demand. But the former is still required at the level of reasonableness, when one asks which of the possibilities envisaged is the most liable to be true, or which contemplated course of action will probably do the most good, on the available evidence. The expert's "homology,"

36. Marx is a case in point, though Freud is not. It would be absurd to accuse the latter of underestimating the strength or the persistence of the unpleasant side of human nature.

when properly justified, rests on the "paralogies" of many inventors; to be in the position essential to the expert, of being able to make well-founded judgments, one must have envisaged the alternatives and know why there is good reason to reject those which have been set aside. Lyotard confuses the principle of noncontradiction, which is essential to reasonable judgment—he himself cannot at the same time be a competent Hungarian speaker and know no Hungarian words at all—with the sort of power-driven ideology where it is the interest of powerful groups, not deference to the relevant evidence, that determines what is to be believed and sought for. This brings us to the paradox that is diagnostic of postmodernism: except insofar as Lyotard's rhetoric at least implictly appeals to evidence as supporting one set of judgments rather than another, it should not convince his readers that anything is so or not so, or ought to be done or ought not to be done. It should certainly be acknowledged that the stimulation of intelligence into action, which is accomplished very well by the kind of writing that Lyotard practises and commends, is a *necessary* condition of rationality; but it is not a *sufficient* condition. You cannot have rationality without it, but you can have it without having rationality. To repeat what is after all a point of the utmost importance—it is one thing to be stimulated or invited to attend to evidence or envisage a range of possibilities, another to be persuaded for good reason that one possibility is to be preferred to others with respect to its truth or goodness. As to the methods of persuasion, there are at least three kinds that have to be distinguished from one another: (1) forcing opinions on people without regard to, or actually in despite of, their own rationality (attentiveness, intelligence, reasonableness); (2) getting people to accept opinions through an invitation to apply their own rationality; and (3) simply placing evidence or a range of different alternatives before them, and leaving them to make judgments entirely by themselves. Lyotard writes as though (1) and

(3) were strict alternatives, and (2) not a genuine possibility. It will be noted that this lack of advertence to the conditions of reasonable judgment is as typical of Foucault and Derrida as it is of Lyotard; it could in fact be said to be characteristic of postmodernism in general.

When it comes to the alleged underivability of prescriptions from descriptions, it is partly amusing, partly very irritating, to find Lyotard parroting that tired and misleading cliché of the Anglo-Saxon philosophy of the last generation. It is true that prescriptions do not follow as a matter of strict deductive logic from descriptions. On the other hand, the suitability or desirability of prescriptions obviously can often be inferred from descriptions, especially those which have implications for happiness and fairness among human beings (and to some extent other sensitive creatures). There is no philosophical mystery about the following little dialogue: "Stop hitting your little sister, Nigel." "Why?" "Because it hurts her." Any normally socialized human being knows that it is a bad thing to hurt other people without good reason (for example, their own greater long-term happiness); anyone who did not know this would hardly know the meaning of "bad."

While the proliferation of language-games is certainly useful for keeping attentiveness and intelligence alive, it does not dispense us from reasonableness. According to the New Enlightenment, while such attentiveness and intelligence are necessary conditions of rationality, they are by no means sufficient conditions. Oversight of this crucial fact might well be said, on a New Enlightenment basis, to be the central shortcoming of Lyotard, from which all the rest are to be derived. Some uses of language are definitely *bad,* if they obstruct the route of human rational authenticity toward apprehension of the true and the good. It was said of South Africa a few years ago that the use of the word "kaffir" as the subject of a sentence implied that nothing polite could be its predicate[37]—and thus the assumption of the inferiority of some races as compared with others was reinforced. When we call things that blow your legs off and leave you screaming "anti-personnel devices," we are indulging in uses of language that are "bad" in this sense. If we call a police officer who is conscientious in the performance of his duties a "pig," it is easier to forget about his pain when we punch him in the face, or not to worry about the fate of his family if he is killed or permanently disabled. To keep attentiveness and intelligence alive is perhaps the most serious purpose of literature and the arts.[38] This is why corrupt regimes resort to extensive censorship of the arts, since the unrestricted play of attentiveness and intelligence may lead to reasonable judgment and responsible action of a kind that is inconvenient to the authorities in such regimes. A novel or play that tends to promote sympathy for the plight of Ruritanians may well be suppressed by a regime motivated to treat Ruritanians with special unfairness or cruelty. What it all comes down to is that there are both cognitive and moral criteria for the assessment of ways of talking; a merely aesthetic criterion, as apparently advocated by Lyotard, is seriously insufficient. Uses of language that tend to promote xenophobia, or the beating-up of homosexuals, can seem much more thrilling and sexy than those which turn a critical eye on such attitudes and practices.

Lyotard denies that "desire" and "life" can be represented. But, so far as these terms bear a meaning anything like their usual one, representation of desire and life is surely possible, at least to some extent. (Of course, on Derridean principles, it may be doubted whether *anything* is capable of representation.)

37. I owe this point to a talk I heard many years ago by Guy Braithwaite, O.P.

38. Cf. Meynell, *The Nature of Aesthetic Value* (Albany, N.Y.: State University of New York Press, 1986), chap. 2.

As I have said already, each of us knows by experience what it is to be relatively happy or sad, fulfilled or frustrated. Thus we can aim for a state of affairs, in our own immediate environment or in human society in general, where happiness is as much enhanced and widely shared as possible, and avoid one where there is substantial injustice and misery. That is to say, we know what it is for "desire" to be more or less fulfilled, "life" more or less enhanced. One may concede to Lyotard that the unsettling of linguistic conventions and the received opinions they express is worthwhile so far as this is a means to more knowledge of the truth and to realization of a greater good.

As I have already tried to show, on New Enlightenment principles one can construct an idea of the good as that ideal blend of happiness and fairness on the basis of which all particular human aims, actions, and policies are to be evaluated. To adopt or adapt Lyotard's terminology, one could call this either the correct metanarrative or the metametanarrative in relation to which particular metanarratives—capitalism, Freudianism, Marxism and so on—are to be evaluated. It is clear enough that justification in terms of such a (meta)metanarrative is implicit in each of these ideologies.[39] For Freud, happiness and fairness among human beings are considerably increased (though he insists, with the grim honesty which is so characteristic of him, that he has no paradise to offer) so far as the unruly and mutually destructive forces of the id (approximately, our raw and uncoordinated instinctive drives) are harmonized and coordinated through the ego (roughly, the conscious mind).[40] For Marx, if present social conflicts are sharpened with revolution as the result, and if this revolution places in power the previously downtrodden majority of people, a hitherto undreamed-of era

39. I use the term here in a neutral rather than a pejorative sense.

40. See Meynell, *Freud, Marx and Morals* (New York: Barnes and Noble, 1981), chap. 5.

of happiness and fairness will ensue once the State, or the mechanism by which one class dominates and represses another, has "withered away."[41] In the capitalist utopia, free enterprise will ensure sufficient goods for the happiness of all, and Adam Smith's "hidden hand" will see to their sufficiently equitable distribution. It may well seem[42] that none of these metanarratives will quite do as it stands, at least without some corrective by the others; it appears that Lyotard himself has been disappointed in his expectations of Marxism and Freudianism, and has consequently turned against metanarratives in general. Certainly, the most influential metanarratives have done a good deal of harm. But Lyotard's suggested cure, of having no articulate moral, social, or political ideals whatever, seems worse than the disease. The solution to the problem is surely to clarify the second-order conception of the idea of the good, as the ideal to which human societies approach so far as happiness and fairness are maximized within them, and to judge practices and first-order ideals accordingly. Unfortunately, as Michael Novak has remarked,[43] ideologists have the bad habit of comparing their own ideals with the actual practice of their opponents. A New Enlightenment comparison would insist, however, that the ideals (for instance, to take Novak's own example) of capitalists and socialists should be compared with one another, and that the actual records of regimes claiming to follow capitalist and socialist ideals should be similarly compared.[44]

41. Ibid., chap. 4. The expression "the withering-away of the State" is in fact due to Engels.

42. It certainly seems so to me, but I do not want to prejudge the issue. It could in principle be the case that one of these metanarratives turned out to be more effective than any other in realizing the idea of the good, given the constraints imposed by human nature. The point is that this is the test any such metanarrative would have to face and to surmount.

43. *The Spirit of Democratic Capitalism* (New York: Simon and Schuster 1982), 26.

44. Cf. the Parable of the Two Sons (Matthew 21:28–31).

Where the good as well as the true is concerned, Lyotard is quite right that a wide variety of points of view should be encouraged and that a lively and experimental attitude to language—the antithesis of the mind-numbing bureaucratic jargon to which contemporary human beings too often subject themselves and others—is an important means to such an end. But, as usual, while Lyotard's proposals are admirable at the level of what the New Enlightenment calls intelligence, they are all at sea when it comes to reasonableness. People may have any number of bright, crazy, well-intentioned, or frightful ideas about how society might be run, but not even all the proposals that are both clever and well intentioned are consistent with one another. And whatever the general desirability of freedom of speech, it is far from obvious that every way of talking should be allowed in every circumstance. In the interests of free speech, some palpable falsehoods, and a few nasty palpable falsehoods at that, have to be permitted to be spoken and written. But can we really preserve whatever good our society may have achieved if, for example, we allow sado-masochistic pornography to be sold to small children, or calumnies against racial or religious minorities to be taught as facts in our schools?

Lyotard is apparently convinced that "consensus politics" is bad, since some forms of consensus lead to injustice. But to say clearly that they are bad is either arbitrary or susceptible of justification. However, it is difficult to see how such justification could be provided except in terms of some kind of metanarrative. Lyotard admits that some situations are unjust; but if there is no principle according to which some are unjust, others not, you might just as well label them one way or the other according to your prejudice or caprice. Lyotard is in fact admirably sensitive to the dangers of injustice. The moment one asks what injustice is, though, and why it ought to be avoided, some sort of metanarrative becomes indispensable. By virtue of the very nature of "good," one might say, human social arrangements are good so far as they foster happiness and justice. Lyotard effectively assumes this, just as nearly everyone else does (as in the case of other postmodernists, common sense and common decency have a way of breaking into his reflections, in spite of everything). It is curious how, when reasons are obvious and taken for granted, we tend not to advert to them. He is quite right, of course, that particular conceptions of what is good, like Marxist revolution or capitalist production, should not themselves be taken as unconditionally good; but he is alarmingly unclear about the basis on which they ought to be criticized.

The "Idea" commended by Lyotard to differentiate his position from sheer conventionalism, so far as one can frame a clear conception of what is involved in it, is totally inadequate for the purpose. Obvious falsehoods, as well as moral abominations, can have a great aesthetic appeal, especially when so many people are oppressed by what Emile Durkheim called the "moral mediocrity"—lack of ideals to touch the heart and make the pulses race—that is such an obvious feature of much modern life.

When one set of ideas is being jettisoned in favor of another—something which on Lyotard's account we should constantly be doing—it is presumably worth asking oneself whether the change is for the better or for the worse. If democratic ways of thinking and acting within a society are replaced by fascist ones, most people, including Lyotard himself, would probably say that the change was for the worse. And it is for the worse for the clearly statable reason that democracies on the whole tend to foster happiness and fairness more than do fascist regimes. There are deceptive and oppressive language-games, as I have already said. If the criterion of preference between them is, as Lyotard seems to suggest, merely aesthetic, a way of speaking that is worse than another from the point of view of the overall human good may well appear more appealing. One must of course agree, in a sense, with Lyotard, that there are no *precise* rules for dealing with interpersonal conflicts, where the interests or apparent interests of two or more persons or groups are at odds with one another. General method, as conceived in New Enlightenment terms, could be said to issue in *principles* rather than *rules* for situations such as this—you should try to understand the opposing point of view, and to put your own clearly and without exaggeration; you should resist and abstain from bullying, and look and see how far compromise is possible. All things being equal, you should avoid hurting and annoying other people; you should behave fairly pleasantly to them, or at least not deliberately offend them except for special reasons. You should conform to social conventions governing situations, except when there is good reason to break them in the light of the idea of the good. Lyotard will not admit such principles because of his extreme libertarianism, which in turn is born of a reaction to tyrannical applications of such inadequate narratives (at least as he and I see it) as Marxism. However, he seems right in suggesting that an imagined state of affairs may be useful as an ideal, even if it could never be realized in practice: a perfectly fair and happy society would seem to function as just such an unrealizable ideal in relation to which actual social arrangements may be evaluated.

Lyotard shares with Foucault the bad habit—which perhaps does more credit to his heart than discredit to his head—of slipping into his arguments implicit normative assumptions that he explicitly denies. Notoriously, there is no *compulsion* imposed on me by the claims of other people. I *can* too easily ride roughshod over another person's claims, refusing to listen to her protests and complaints, however well justified they are, so long as I can get away with it. An academic invites a junior colleague to lunch to discuss topics of mutual interest, expecting as a matter of course acceptance or polite refusal of the invitation. She aggressively and sarcastically dismisses the request as inappropriate. When, more in surprise than in anger, he tries to find out why she is so uncivil, she complains to their Head of Department, and it goes into his file at the Dean's office that he has been harassing her. What is wrong with that kind of behavior? Simply that it violates norms that must be obeyed by most members of any community that is to achieve and maintain a tolerable level of happiness and fairness among its members. But this does not imply that there is any "necessity" about her behaving any better, so long as she can get away with behaving as she does.

Richard Rorty remarks that Habermas has sought to ground in a more inclusive theory the attempts by Marx and Freud to lay bare the ideology and wish-fulfilment that dictate so much human thought and action. He adds that Lyotard, as contrasted with Habermas, is suspicious of these "masters of suspicion" themselves. (In this paragraph and the following two, I shall summarize, without commentary, Rorty's account of the contrast between Habermas and Lyotard.) Lyotard actually describes it as characteristic of modernity to try to justify its claims by appeal to some philosophical metadiscourse or grand narrative. He describes postmodernism as incredulous toward all such justifications. In Habermas' opinion, however, the unmasking of ideology can be intelligible only on the basis of the preservation of at least one overriding standard. Short of this, he maintains, rational criticism of existing beliefs and institutions becomes impossible, and all that is left is unprincipled and *ad hoc* negation. As a consequence, "we find French critics of Habermas trying to hang on to universalistic philosophy, with all its problems, in order to support liberal politics."[45] (Rorty for his part will champion the liberal politics while dispensing with the universalistic philosophy.)

45. See R. Rorty, "Habermas and Lyotard on Postmodernism," in *Habermas on Modernity*, ed. Richard J. Bernstein (Cambridge: Polity Press, 1985), 161–62.

Lyotard attacks Habermas for wanting to regularize all the possible rules in language-games, in the interests of the emancipation of humanity. He himself sees consensus as a mere stage in science, the aim of which is "paralogy."[46] The grounds for this curious view (as Rorty understandably finds it to be) seems to be, in part at least, that postmodern science concerns itself with conflicts, catastrophes, and paradoxes, and so itself aspires to be conflictual, catastrophic, and paradoxical.[47] He seems to be maintaining, in effect, that science aims at permanent revolution, rather than being characterized by that alternation of normality and revolution which has been made familiar by Thomas Kuhn. However, to say, as Lyotard does, that the aim of science is to heap paralogy on paralogy, is rather like saying that the aim of politics is to heap revolution on revolution—it is a gross misrepresentation of how things are (or of how any sensible person thinks that they ought to be). "The most that could be shown is that talk of the aims of either [i.e., politics or science] is not particularly useful."[48]

Still, Lyotard does have a point, which he shares with Mary Hesse in her criticism of Habermas' distinction between natural and human science. Hesse maintains that Anglo-Saxon post-empiricist philosophy of science has shown "that the language of theoretical science is irreducibly metaphorical and unformalizable, and that the logic of science is circular interpretation, re-interpretation, and self-correction of data in terms of theory, theory in terms of data."[49] Lyotard also wants, quite correctly in Rorty's view, to mitigate the positivist dichotomy between science on the one hand, which is supposed to be justified by rigorous methodological criteria, and nonscientific types of

46. Lyotard, *Postmodern,* 65–66. 47. Ibid., 60.
48. Rorty, "Habermas," 163.
49. Mary Hesse, *Revolutions and Reconstructions in the Philosophy of Science* (Bloomington, Ind.: Indiana University Press, 1980), 173.

"knowledge" and activity on the other. Apparently, so far as Lyotard is concerned, "the trouble with Habermas is not so much that he provides a metanarrative of emancipation as that he feels the need to legitimize, that he is not content to let the narratives which hold our culture together do their stuff. He is scratching where it does not itch." Several American commentators on Habermas, while generally sympathetic to his point of view, also "doubt that studies of communicative competence can do what transcendental philosophy failed to do in the way of providing 'universalistic' criteria." And Rorty finds their doubts well founded. But he insists that it is a mistake to be bothered by the failure, which merely goes to show what should never have been attempted in the first place. We think that there is a problem here "only because an overzealous philosophy of science has created an impossible ideal of ahistorical legitimation." We should embrace Lyotard's scepticism toward "metanarratives" while eschewing his curious insistence that intellectuals must be "avant-garde," with its silly "Leftist" assumption that one is "compromised" if one promotes consensus between and communication with already existing institutions. As to the "disenchantment of the world" that so many have lamented as characteristic of the modern era, we would do well to heed John Dewey's suggestion, that immersion in immediate and concrete practical concerns, "the meaning of the daily detail" as he put it, will give us back whatever it was that our ancestors found in religion.[50]

The mistaken nature of the quest for legitimation is one of the main points at issue in *Philosophy and the Mirror of Nature,*[51] where Rorty attacks a belief or assumption that has dominated Western philosophy since the seventeenth century (and argua-

50. Rorty, "Habermas," 164–65, 174–76.

51. R. Rorty, *Philosophy and the Mirror of Nature* (Princeton: Princeton University Press, 1979).

bly long before)—that the human mind reflects or pictures nature, or rather can be made to do so by following the appropriate procedures. Philosophers, says Rorty, retained a special position in the academy, at any rate in their own estimation, so long as they could think of themselves as the authorities on these procedures. Some eighty to ninety years ago, however, philosophers were afflicted with an identity crisis, when the suspicion became colorable that there would soon be nothing left of their specialty. The natural scientists had taken charge of knowledge of the physical world some centuries earlier; now psychologists and sociologists were invading the territory of the human "mind," which indeed, as was coming increasingly to be realized, was nothing over and above the human brain and human dispositions to behavior. The writing on the wall for philosophy, at least as traditionally conceived, is even clearer now.[52]

On this crucial issue of the supposed "foundations of knowledge," the commonly accepted division between "Anglo-Saxon" or "analytic" philosophy on the one hand, and "Continental," "phenomenological" or "existentialist" philosophy on the other, does not apply. Bertrand Russell and Edmund Husserl, from their very different points of view, were convinced that knowledge had foundations, and they tried to set out what they were. Their followers Ludwig Wittgenstein and Martin Heidegger realized that this was a mistake, and the American John Dewey arrived at similar conclusions. The fact is, according to Rorty, that there is no theory of knowledge to be had, other than what can be provided in principle by psychologists and sociologists, who can tell us a causal story about how people arrive at beliefs which are dignified by the honorific title "true," and at ways of behavior that are commended by calling them "good." To ask whether the behavior is *really* good, whether our society commends it or not, is to appeal to nonexistent stan-

52. Ibid., 12, 165.

dards supposed somehow to transcend societies. Likewise, to ask whether the beliefs are *really* "true" is to presuppose that our "minds" are after all actual or potential "mirrors of nature," and so might reflect it more accurately than they did in the past or do at present.[53] As soon ask whether a young woman and man are really married, when it is admitted that they have gone through all the rigmarole accepted in their society as bringing a marriage into being.

The "foundations" of knowledge, like the "foundations" of culture in general, do not exist; it is a waste of time to go on looking for them. Scientists engage in one kind of activity that happens to be valued in our culture, just as politicians and musicians engage in other kinds. The notion that their activities have or need to have "foundations," about which philosophers might spend their time dictating to them, has turned out to be an illusion. Rorty tries to show that all attempts to find such "foundations" have ended in failure. If philosophers give up their bogus pretensions to intellectual hegemony, that does not mean that they need be out of a job. They may devote themselves instead to the comparatively humble, yet useful and agreeable task, of promoting conversation between different human groups, especially when these groups encounter problems of mutual understanding.[54]

In considering Rorty's position, the reader may care to attend to the following valid argument:

If there is no sound transcendental philosophy, some substitute is needed to justify alleged "knowledge" and "culture" as really being such.

But there is no sound transcendental philosophy.

Therefore some substitute is needed to justify alleged "knowledge" and "culture" as really being such.

53. Ibid., 8, 211; chapter 5.

54. Ibid., 11–12, 168, 187.

Habermas accepts both premisses and conclusion of the argument, and his principal philosophical effort has been devoted to trying to find such a substitute. His critics argue—in my view, correctly—that his attempt, though unquestionably impressive, ultimately fails. Representatives of the New Enlightenment, maintaining as they do that there is a sound transcendental philosophy, can avoid the conclusion because they reject the second premiss. Rorty rejects the first premiss: we have "narratives" within our culture that "do their stuff," and they should be left to do it. But the narratives are palpably *not* doing their stuff. Many people reject the values of liberal democracy, and many others wonder how they can be defended, if at all. In this situation, it is difficult to sit down under the bland assurance that, while liberal democracy cannot be justified, there is no need to worry about this. Many people feel the itch intensely and are vigorously scratching, however much Rorty tells them that, since there is no itch, there is no need to scratch. And it is notable that Rorty himself makes it of the essence of his pragmatism that one makes suggestions as to how affairs could be run *better* than they are. But, on Rorty's principles, "this is how we might run things better" amounts to no more than "This is how I propose to run things"—unless those in his society, or perhaps just its most prestigious or vociferous members, already agree with him, in which case there is little point in making the proposal.[55] As for the "narratives" alluded to by Rorty and Lyotard, either they just reassert the values in question, or they provide some attempt at justification. Rorty denies that such justification is necessary or ultimately possible. But merely to reiterate one's adherence to the values does nothing but confirm in their convictions those who are already convinced anyway.

55. For similar objections, see Hilary Putnam, *Realism with a Human Face* (Cambridge: MIT Press, 1991), 23–24.

On the principles of the New Enlightenment, it is easy, at least in principle, to justify liberal democracy as the best way yet devised of maximizing within a society the ultimate values of happiness and fairness. This is hardly compatible with the perpetual unrest and ferment that seem to be recommended by Lyotard. As Aristotle pointed out long ago, the good life cannot be lived in conditions of what he called "stasis,"[56] when not only can you not rely on the paper and the milk arriving daily on your doorstep, but you may well be in frequent danger of death. Rorty commends—he admits that he cannot justify—the liberal ideal of public tolerance and private freedom, where each is encouraged to direct her own life so far as possible, provided that she does no harm to other people. This, again, is easy to justify on New Enlightenment principles. If authentic human living is a matter of being comprehensively attentive, intelligent, reasonable, and responsible, it will not be achieved in a society where persons are allowed to bully others or forced to submit to bullies, or where people are ordered about more than is necessary to preserve a tolerable degree of social harmony. Rorty has New Enlightenment instincts; it is a pity that he cannot see his way to the principles that would justify them.

Rorty denies that the human "mind" is the "mirror of nature," a view that he maintains has been held, at least in the main, by the Western philosophical tradition, more especially since Descartes. Now it is obviously wrong to say that the mind is literally a mirror in which the external world of shoes, ships, and sealing-wax is reflected. It is scarcely less evidently wrong to claim that we have got to know of the existence and nature of transuranic elements and pterosaurs just by passively exposing our minds to their influence. But it is one thing to make

56. He says, with his usual good sense, that *stasis* is more likely in circumstances of gross inequity in distribution of wealth. Cf. *Politics* IV, 9, 1295a36–1296a1.

these two admissions, quite another to deny that, by an appropriate exercise of our minds and our sensory apparatus, we can get to know about a world of things and events that exists and is as it is largely prior to and independently of ourselves. And this is exactly what Rorty does appear to deny. The extreme oddness of this position is softened by Rorty's rhetoric, which may make it difficult for some people to see the grossly implausible consequences of his position for what they are. As anyone but a consistent subjective idealist would see it, red-giant stars shone, mammal blood circulated, and birds migrated many millions of years before any human beings got to know that they did. So far as we know that these things are so, when most earlier human generations did not, there is a clear sense in which our minds "reflect" how things are more than theirs did, are more comprehensive and accurate "mirrors of nature." Does Rorty really wish to deny that the states of affairs mentioned were the case before anyone came to know that they were, and yet that people did come to know that they were? Dr. Stanley Stein has suggested to me that Rorty would try to "prevent such a question from arising." One can only reply with Northrop Frye's comment, that the reaction of a healthy mind, when told not to ask a question, is to ask it all the more insistently. If Rorty's denial that the mind is the mirror of nature does not have the bizarre consequences I have suggested, he has not made it clear what it amounts to.

Furthermore, it does not seem in the least difficult to spell out in general terms *why* we are confident that the states of affairs mentioned are the case, and so the beliefs we hold about them are true, in spite of the fact that so many of our predecessors were ignorant of them. There were many data of possible experience to which they had not attended, questions they had not asked, and possibilities they had not envisaged. They were thus in no position to make the relevant judgments even tentatively, let alone as confidently as we can make them. The New Enlightenment, in common with many thinkers of the Old (notably Kant), in fact directly affirms an epistemological thesis which Rorty explicitly denies—that the foundations of knowledge consist of two components, the data of experience and an a priori structure provided by the mind.[57] We assume them by instinct and can get to know them strictly speaking—that is, form true beliefs for good reason about them—by the sort of philosophical reflection sponsored by the New Enlightenment.

According to Rorty, to say that a statement is true, or that an action is good, is no more than to commend it as approved in our culture. But for all the remarkable skill with which Rorty camouflages the fact, the consequences of this position are bizarre in the extreme. Does he really want to deny that the planet Neptune, with the characteristics and properties that our astronomers attribute to it, existed before there were human astronomers; or that human beings within certain cultures have found out what was really so about it, and that their statements are true so far as they state those things which are thus so? Yet to assert all these propositions seems flagrantly inconsistent with Rorty's view that there are no "transcendent" standards of truth or of rationality (as the means par excellence of getting at such truth), that there are only statements and methods that our culture happens to commend by calling them "true" and rational. The truth of statements about the planet Neptune depends on what is the case about the planet Neptune, and not on rules and conventions observed in our society. To be rational about the planet Neptune is a matter of following procedures that are liable to lead to such truth.

I must note that Jürgen Habermas has made objections to postmodernism that are in some ways parallel to my own. I

57. Cf. Rorty, *Philosophy,* 168, 180.

have discussed Habermas at some length in another book[58] and see no good reason to repeat myself here. Roughly and summarily, Habermas' position is an unstable compromise. On the one hand, he wants to repudiate anything that smacks of "first philosophy"; on the other, he insists, in the manner of Enlightenments Old and New, on comprehensive criticism of factual beliefs, moral attitudes, and self-consciousness. These stances are not compatible with each other. The former issues in postmodernism when followed through consistently, the latter in the principles that, as is shown in my second chapter, are central to the New Enlightenment. These certainly amount to a 'first philosophy' in the sense intended by Habermas.

Omission of a consideration of Ludwig Wittgenstein, in a study of postmodernism, may well strike some readers as tantamount to Hamlet without the prince. Now exegesis of Wittgenstein is a heavy industry, in the machinery of which it is very unwise for nonspecialists to get entangled. And it is pretty clear what the four postmodernists whom I have selected as typical were trying to say, while the question of what Wittgenstein was really getting at is notoriously obscure and controversial.[59] Lengthy preoccupation with it would unbalance this book as a whole, distracting the reader from the main issues with which it tries to deal. I shall accordingly take an account of Wittgenstein's thought which I find plausible, the masterly one by Anthony Quinton,[60] and base a very short discussion on that. Briefly and roughly, it may be said that an extreme and some-

58. *Redirecting Philosophy* (Toronto: University of Toronto Press, 1998), chapter 11.

59. Shadia Drury has remarked caustically, in conversation, that analytical philosophers are inclined to dismiss many remarks of Foucault as absurd but pay reverential attention when Wittgenstein says what is apparently just the same thing.

60. See the "Extract from Modern British Philosophy" in G. Pitcher, ed., *Wittgenstein: The Philosophical Investigations* (London: Macmillan, 1968).

what idiosyncratic application of the principles of the Old Enlightenment is to be found in Wittgenstein's early thought, as represented by the *Tractatus Logico-Philosophicus*[61] and as influential on the Logical Positivists. Postmodernism is at least strongly anticipated in the *Philosophical Investigations,*[62] and it becomes rampant in *On Certainty.*[63]

According to the *Tractatus,* "elementary" propositions[64] are true or false by virtue of "picturing"[65] or failing to picture the "elementary facts" that make up the world.[66] (These elementary facts were interpreted by the Logical Positivists as sense experiences; but while Wittgenstein seems for a time to have come round to this view later, it is not strictly implied by what is said in the *Tractatus.*) In the case of all other meaningful propositions, their truth or falsity is a matter of the truth or falsity of elementary propositions—in Wittgenstein's terminology, they are "truth-functions" of them.[67] All other utterances that appear to be propositions lack significance strictly speaking, and three types of these are in effect distinguished by Wittgenstein. First and most deplorable are the pseudo-propositions of metaphysics, which unfortunately make up a large part of traditional philosophy. Second, there are the quasi-propositions exemplified by what is said in the *Tractatus* itself.[68] To put the matter succinctly, a discourse that explains how all meaningful propositions are either elementary propositions that picture elementary facts, or truth-functions thereof, cannot itself consist of such propositions. Thirdly and lastly, there are the profundities

61. Wittgenstein, *Tractatus Logico-Philosophicus* (London: Routledge and Kegan Paul, 1961; first published 1921).

62. Oxford: Blackwell, 1958; first published 1953.

63. Oxford: Blackwell, 1969. This consists of notes that Wittgenstein made shortly before his death in 1951.

64. *Tractatus* 4.21.

65. Ibid., 4.01.

66. Ibid., 1.1.

67. Ibid., 5.

68. Ibid., 6.54.

of the "mystical" as expressed apparently in the language of morality and religion.[69]

Wilfred Sellars has referred to the *Tractatus* as a "jewel box of insights."[70] From the point of view of the New Enlightenment, it might rather be described as a Pandora's box of oversights. By the time he came to write the *Philosophical Investigations,* Wittgenstein seems to have come to believe this himself. In this work, language is compared to a toolbox containing tools for doing different things,[71] in implied contrast with the principal thing, representing or "picturing" the facts of the world, which is harped on by the *Tractatus.* Words and phrases are described in their association with social and practical activities: we read of builders in gangs shouting "slab" to one another while they work at passing slabs and putting them in place.[72] "Ask not for the meaning, ask for the use."[73] One is invited to look at utterances in context, rather than pursuing the will-o'-the-wisp of what they "mean"—as though this were something "private" and interior to the "mind." "An expression has meaning only within the stream of life"; hence the aptness of the injunction, "Don't think, but look."[74] Obviously connected with these concerns and preoccupations is the behaviorist flavor of the whole, and the hostility evinced to the notion of a "private language."[75]

What the *Philosophical Investigations* fails to draw attention to—one might say, this was not its job, which was to supply a corrective to the opposite exaggeration—is that "language

69. Ibid., 6.44, 6.45, 6.522.

70. W. Sellars, *Science, Perception and Reality* (London: Routledge and Kegan Paul, 1963), 215.

71. Wittgenstein, *Investigations* 11. The reference is not to pages but to numbered entries.

72. Ibid., 2, 10, 19–21.

73. On "meaning" and "use," see ibid., 43.

74. Ibid., 66.

75. Ibid., 243, 256.

games"[76] and the "forms of life"[77] that they make up characteristically depend on assumptions both about what is the case and about what is worthwhile. The builders in Wittgenstein's example assume that their slabs are of suitable material to make buildings, as sufficiently rigid, durable, and capable of taking strain; and that enough money will be made available by their employers for the maintenance of themselves and their families in an adequate way of life. It is such assumptions as these that make it seem worthwhile for them to do the work that includes the language-game in question. And it seems obvious that one can ask how far such assumptions are well- or ill-founded. Much the same applies, I would say, on the large scale as on the small, even to religious doctrines and the rituals and ethical practices associated with them: they state or presuppose that what determines the world and human fate is of one nature rather than another, and this justifies and makes appropriate and worthwhile various practices and ways of talking that would not otherwise be so. And one may ask whether such beliefs about the world and human fate, and what lies behind them, are themselves justified. But this consideration, of course, heads toward the view of the Old and New Enlightenments, that general principles of justification are available that can and ought to be applied to all questions, including, perhaps especially, the most fundamental.

One may well infer from the notes made by Wittgenstein shortly before his death, published as *On Certainty,* that all justification is within a system;[78] that such systems depend on how we act more than on anything else;[79] and that the ways of

76. Ibid., 7, 23. 77. Ibid., 19, 23.

78. Wittgenstein, *Certainty* 105, 410. The references are once again to the numbered entries. The reader will please note that my interpretation of *On Certainty,* as of the other works of Wittgenstein to which I have referred, is studiously guarded.

79. Ibid., 110, 204.

acting and the systems that depend on them differ radically from place to place and from time to time.[80] This seems to be a thoroughly postmodern position, implying as it does denial of the conviction constitutive of both Old and New Enlightenments, that there are principles of justification, cognitive and perhaps evaluative, that transcend the contingencies and vicissitudes of particular human societies and their customs.

80. Ibid., 336.

5

THE COMET'S TAIL

THE PSYCHOANALYST Felix Guattari, in a piece significantly entitled "The Postmodern Dead End," remarks that "[a] certain idea of modernity and progress has gone bankrupt, and in its fall it has dragged along all confidence in the notion of emancipation through social action." At the same time economic inequities have solidified, unemployment and poverty are put up with as unavoidable, and the viewpoint of the workers' supposed representatives has become hardly distinguishable from that of the technocrats.[1] It is difficult to disagree with him. The solution is, first, to work out a comprehensively critical conception of the good—and so of human emancipation as an aspect of it—and second, to consider the most effective way to implement it. The former, as I have already argued at length, is supplied by the New Enlightenment; the latter can be achieved only by a long process of trial and error, which uses the insights and corrects the oversights of pioneers like Plato, Aristotle, Marx, Nietzsche, and Freud.[2] Postmodernism as gen-

1. *Flash Art* 28, May/June 1986, 40. See J. Pefanis, *Heterology and the Postmodern: Bataille, Baudrillard and Lyotard* (Durham, N.C., and London: Duke University Press, 1991), 6–7.

2. I have tried to show how this might be done in *Freud, Marx and Morals* (New York: Barnes and Noble, 1981).

erally understood, and as exemplified in the work of most of the the authors discussed so far, is clearly not only incapable of meeting the former requirement, but in principle destructive of all efforts to meet it. However, it has rendered the useful service of pointing to limitations or inadequacies in the methods and assumptions characteristic of the Old Enlightenment. Guattari goes on to ask whether we really have to "remain passive in the face of a rising wave of cruelty and cynicism," which "would seem to be the deplorable conclusion to which many intellectual and artistic groups have come, especially those who claim the banner of postmodernism." This "deplorable conclusion," of course, would be quite unnecessary if only we could obtain a distinct notion of what would be unequivocally *better* than what we have at present. But unfortunately it is of the essence of postmodernism, with its destructive approach to all "metanarratives" and their associated norms, to subvert all such notions.

Lyotard is one specific target of Guattari's criticisms; another is Jean Baudrillard. Baudrillard is vehemently opposed to the modern obsession with production. As he sees it, objects before the modern era were "heavy" with significance, however useless; the modern functional object is "light," useful but insignificant. Extreme rationality turns itself into irrationality, such that (in Julian Pefanis's words) "production produces in order to produce production." Non-Western societies are infected by the omnipresent miasma; as Pierre Clastres puts it, they are faced with the alternative of producing or perishing, of being subjected to ethnocide or genocide.[3] Meanwhile the Western public, by means of what has been called "consumer engineering," is habituated to planned obsolescence in the goods it purchases, and has come to assume that it has a natural right to the unlimited consumption of products. One important motive that

3. Pierre Clastres, *Recherches d'anthropologie politique* (Paris: Seuil, 1980), 56.

drives the consumer, on Baudrillard's view, is social distinction; in fact progress, in modern capitalist society, consists in the reduction of all other values to production that promotes either social distinction or financial profit.[4] Language gets impoverished accordingly, and the many denunciations of the trend in effect collude with it. As Pefanis puts it, "The critique itself is implicated as the accomplice of the object of criticism." In Baudrillard's own words, "Just as the society of the middle ages equilibrated itself on God AND Devil, so ours equilibrates itself on consumption AND its denunciation."[5]

The New Enlightenment is neither at the feet nor at the throat of production. Rather it asks how far the exercise of our unprecendented power to produce, and so to transform the human environment, really and in the long term contributes to the overall good. It is by now notorious that the envisagement of the earth exclusively as raw material for production and consumption not only is deadening to the human spirit, but will lead sooner rather than later to ecological disaster. Here the correctives supplied by authors like Baudrillard are useful, if not taken to an excess worse than the ills they are supposed to remedy. We need and ought to produce, but clear-sightedly and in moderation, and with an articulate view of the good to be gained by it. Baudrillard is also to be commended for shrewdly bringing out the difference between the kind of criticism that merely provides a cultured *frisson* for the beneficiaries of established assumptions and fashions, in the manner of a court jester, and a genuinely subversive engagement with them.[6] But a truly effective criticism depends

4. Jean Baudrillard, *La société de consommation* (Paris: Gallimard, 1970), 75.

5. Ibid., 315–16. Pefanis, *Heterology*, 7, 25, 61–62, 64, 66–67, 70.

6. I was told by my friend and former colleague Roger White that there were three parties in the Lutheran Church in East Germany under the former Communist government, two of them legal, one illegal. One legal party applauded as a matter of course everything that was said or done by the government, the other deplored it. It was easy to dismiss the latter as a mere lackey of the capitalist West. The illegal party was more discriminating, praising the

on a coherent account of a real good to be achieved and real evils to be avoided, which, as I have already insisted, is impossible within the limits of what is usually called postmodernism. As to the suggestion that an extreme rationality tends to destroy itself, on the New Enlightenment view, as I have already argued, the trouble with a technologically obsessed "rationality" is that it is not rational *enough* to envisage the human good in a sufficiently generalized and undistorted way. As used often to be pointed out a few years ago, there is a substantial difference between "standard of living" and quality of life.

Boris Frankel, in a superb essay, has expressed what must be the reaction of many serious contemporary intellectuals to postmodernism. As he sees it, modernism has unfortunately brought many evils in its train, for all the outstanding benefits it has bestowed on humankind.[7] Postmodernism has responded by an onslaught on the rationality that undergirds not only the worst but also the best in modernism. The logical issue of this (whether it is actually inferred by all who would call themselves postmodernists or not) is a cynical scepticism or relativism and an ideological situation in which democracy cannot be argued to be preferable to tyranny, or freedom to oppression. What other options are left to us? Some would replace the Enlightenment demand for social justice and political liberation with the invitation to personal expression and deliverance from "hang-ups," while others would condemn this as "the culture of narcissism." There is something to be said for both points of view. How to find an acceptable or viable compromise between them is among the most serious of contemporary moral problems. Preoccupation with her inner feelings or development of her

---

government when there seemed to be good reason, and blaming it when there seemed to be good reason. This was too subversive to be acceptable.

7. B. Frankel, "The Cultural Contradictions of Postmodernity," in A. Milner, P. Thomson, and C. Worth, eds., *Postmodern Conditions* (Oxford and Providence, R.I.: Berg Publishers, 1990).

sensibilities may render a person unable or unwilling to cope with the difficulties of living in the world as it is,[8] let alone doing something to alleviate its crying evils and injustices. On the other hand, the puritanical, repressed, and patriarchal individual who provided the traditional moral ideal will hardly be disposed to work for, much less to live in, a society where people are encouraged to care for one another, to be alive to each other's feelings, and to work for or maintain justice between races, economic groups, and the sexes.[9]

It would be widely agreed now that Marxism, which was probably the most thoroughgoing attempt to apply the supposed insights of modernism to society as a whole, has proved a failure, at least in the forms in which it has so far been implemented. Its promises for the future have been replaced, in many minds, by either of two mutually contradictory utopian visions. One, which is typical of environmentalists and some left-wing and anarchistic groups, recommends an out-and-out rejection of modernity, along with a repudiation of technology, the satisfaction of only basic material needs, and small communities all of whose members are in face-to-face relationship with one another. At the other extreme is the demand for an even greater acceleration of technological development, and yet more social diversification and fragmentation; the attendant alienation and distress—even though they result at present in a regular epidemic of violence, addiction, and suicide—will either sort themselves out in time or turn out to be a price worth paying. Some would say that the solution, or part of it, is to revive among people a sense of the sacred;[10] others repudiate this sug-

8. "How can it [the human subject] be strong enough to move in a world founded on injustice? Is it humane to form soft selves in a hard world?" (Richard Sennett, *The Fall of Public Man* [Cambridge: Cambridge University Press 1977], 260; cited in Frankel, "Contradictions," 106).

9. Frankel, "Contradictions," 103–4, 106.

10. Cf. Daniel Bell, *The Cultural Contradictions of Capitalism* (New York: Basic Books, 1978).

gestion;[11] while others still doubt whether it is really possible to repair a sacred canopy that has been torn to shreds.[12] But, as Frankel says, "the demise of religious traditions surely necessitates some concern about the secular values which could possibly unite people in their diversity."[13]

I am not quite happy with the term "socialism" because of the baggage that it carries with it. Entrepreneurs of the kind traditionally applauded by capitalism, who are willing to take risks that will benefit everyone if they are successful, have to be encouraged and rewarded. The crucial question is how they can be so, without the lazy, the feckless, and the merely unfortunate (risks, by definition, may after all fail to come off) going to the wall, together with their dependants. If a non-Marxist "socialism" can include this traditional concern of capitalism, encouraging people to "better" themselves by exercising their talents for the good of society at large, I am perfectly content with it. The ideal society is one that promotes both the production and the distribution of goods of all kinds; where hierarchies exist only insofar as they are genuinely useful;[14] where alienating labor is fairly shared; where people are content with a sustainable enjoyment of material things; and where they are disposed as much as possible to cultivate mutually enhancing human relationships, and as little as possible to hurt, control, or bully one another.

Winston Churchill declared that every society needed both ladders and nets. He meant by this that people ought to be able to benefit themselves and their dependants by the full exercise of their capacities, but that their misfortune, or even their folly, should not consign them too easily to starvation, death by expo-

11. Cf. Alvin Toffler, *The Third Wave* (London: Pan Books, 1980).

12. Thus J. Casanova, "The Politics of Religious Revival," *Telos* (1984), 33: "The experience of the sacred presupposes a sacred cosmos. But can such a cosmos be reconstructed once it has been broken?"

13. Frankel, "Contradictions," 96, 104.

14. For the view that some hierarchies are useful, see pp. 67–68 above.

sure, or lack of the basic amenities of life. The tendency of the "right" is to assume that if the necessary ladders are in place, the nets will look after themselves; of the "left" to maintain that if adequate nets are available, one need not worry much about the ladders. The New Enlightenment, it seems to me, ought to make a priority of the question, "Since we have to see to both the nets and the ladders, how can we get the proportion between them right, or at least less than drastically wrong?"

It is not merely an error, but a dangerous one, to identify with narcissism the disposition to attend to one's consciousness and its operations. On the contrary, if I am aware of my own anger, desire, and fear, and have some notion of the way that they affect my perceptions and decisions, I will be the more able to arrive at true judgments about the needs and feelings of other people, and so to act for the best. When it was suggested to C. G. Jung, that preoccupation with the workings of his own mind was the very last thing that should be demanded of a self-absorbed neurotic, he replied with a memorable comparison. One should not, he said, confuse the flounderings of a drowning person with the purposeful movements of a diver, for all that they may seem superficially to have in common.

The more conscious we are of our own motives, the more usefully we can ask that most important of general contemporary questions about the proper conduct of human life: How may we combine the benefits of modern *Gesellschaft* with those of traditional *Gemeinschaft?* How are we most effectively to reconcile the new freedoms made possible by the (old) Enlightenment and the technology it has produced, with the needs for community and intimate relationships that are inevitable in a species that has evolved within fairly small groups over millions of years? Whatever the ultimate verdict on Marxism, it would be a mistake not to avail ourselves of the useful hints left by Marx himself. He argued that the earlier stages of industrialism had led to a characteristic pattern of alienation and oppression, where owners have exploited workers for their own (actual or supposed) benefit. With the later developments of productive industry, he thought, these forms of oppression and exploitation would be obviously pointless, and a new kind of cooperation and companionship between human beings would become possible.[15] At least something analogous to Marx's communism should in principle be available to us in future. With technology and human science both sufficiently advanced, is there not some ground for hope that a fairly satisfactory compromise will in time be achieved between social needs and values on the one hand and modern opportunities on the other, and between the reward of merit and overall social justice?

What is to be said in general terms about the need for meaning in human life and the revival or reconstitution of the sense of the sacred? Rationalism as conceived by the (old) Enlightenment does seem, at least for a large number of people, to be inimical to religion and to the human needs and longings that were met by it. Is New Enlightenment rationalism also destructive of the sacred, whether for better or worse? I shall have something to say later in this chapter about its bearings on theism, and so on theistic religion. If it were friendly in principle to religion, there would remain the practical problem of hiow to remove traditional moral monstrosities and irrelevancies from religious practice, and to apply it to real improvements in individual and social life as conceived in the light of the idea of the good. (It is obvious enough that there is biblical precedent for this, going back at least to the prophet Amos in the eighth century B.C.E.) If the New Enlightenment were not supportive of any sort of religion, one might wonder to what extent it would be possible, in the manner of Auguste Comte, to apply

15. On what seems to be of permanent value in Marx, see Hugo Meynell, *Freud, Marx and Morals* (New York: Barnes and Noble, 1981), 101–3.

quasi-religious symbolism directly to the needs of society. However, it is rather questionable how far this is practicable as a matter of deliberate social policy; perhaps whatever it is that performs the role of traditional religions within society cannot be manufactured to order.

I have said a good deal about the dearth of basic cognitive and moral norms that characerizes postmodernism. This certainly seems to vitiates the supposed alliance between postmodernism and feminism. The assumption underlying all sane feminism, so far as a male sympathiser can judge, is that women have been subjected to grave injustice in a number of ways due simply to the fact that they are women. If, as I have already argued at some length, the basic criteria of the good are happiness and fairness, then feminism is good because and insofar as it delineates, and sets itself to ameliorate, a situation that is unfair, in that vast numbers of people are barred, for no reason except that they are women, from the happiness and fulfilment of which they are by nature capable.[16] But such an account of the justification of feminism, of course, is not available within the ambit of postmodernism. Also, feminism is surely essentially a movement on behalf of the self-realization of women; and I have no idea how this is to be reconciled with the typical postmodernist view, that there is no self to realize.

According to Rosemarie Tong,[17] postmodern feminists seek to provide a radical criticism of the dominant order, particularly

16. This is the essence of what Christina Hoff Sommers calls "equity feminism," which she usefully distinguishes from "gender feminism" (*Who Stole Feminism?* [New York: Simon and Schuster, 1994]). The latter, which is unfortunately politically fashionable, is well described by Daphne Patai and Noretta Koertge in *Professing Feminism. Cautionary Tales from the Strange World of Women's Studies* (New York: Basic Books, 1994).

17. "Postmodern Feminism"; chap. 8 of Tong, *Feminist Thought* (Boulder, Colo., and San Francisco: Westview Press, 1989). I have depended heavily on Tong's account for this sketch of postmodernist feminism.

in its patriarchal aspects. They admit that this is difficult, when the only words and concepts available for the task were issued by this very order. Also, they wish to avoid making a stanard type of truth-claim, let alone commit themselves to a metaphysical position of the traditional kind. This makes some of them reject any label at all; such labels, it is felt, inevitably evince the "phallologocentric drive to stabilize, organize and rationalize our conceptual universe."[18] Simone de Beauvoir wondered why woman was the "second sex," assuming that "second" was not the best thing to be. Postmodern feminists are apt to reverse the priorities here, emphasizing the special advantage that women have in being able to criticize the reigning patriarchal culture from a position of relative independence.[19]

Hélène Cixous is primarily a novelist, expressing her point of view through experiments in style. Under the baleful influence of masculine speaking and writing, she says, "thought has always worked . . . through dual, hierarchical oppositions,"[20] one of which is always privileged over the other. In "Sorties," she mentions a number of these, such as activity and passivity, sun and moon, culture and nature. All of them are inspired by the fundamental dichotomy of man and woman, where man is assumed to be active, light, and so on—generally positive; and woman passive, dark and so on—generally negative. Cixous wants women to write themselves out of the world that men have made for them, where they are either man's "other," or not thought of at all. She sees close connections between the sexuality of each sex and its writing—male sexuality being

18. Toril Moi, *Sexual/Textual Politics: Feminist Literary Theory* (New York: Methuen 1985), 130–31.

19. Tong, "Feminism," 219, 223.

20. Hélène Cixous and Catherine Clement, "Sorties," in Betsy Wing, trans., *The Newly Born Woman* (Minneapolis: University of Minnesota Press, 1986), 63, 65.

fundamentally boring in its pointed singularity,[21] while feminine sexuality, so far from being boring, is a vast and exciting field which has hardly been explored. "Almost everything is yet to be written by women about femininity: about their sexuality, that is, its infinite and mobile complexity; about their eroticization, sudden turn-ons of a certain minuscule-immense area of their bodies; . . . about the adventure of such and such a drive, about . . . abrupt and gradual awakenings, discoveries of a zone at one time timorous and soon to be forthright."[22]

Cixous is leery of terms like "feminist" and "lesbian," which she finds parasitic on phallologocentric thought in that they imply "deviation from a norm instead of a free sexual option or a place of solidarity with women."[23] Men go on writing what they have written before with their phallic little pens.[24] They like sharp definitions and rigid structures, fear multiplicity and chaos, and are more or less incapable of movement or change. Feminine writing, by contrast, is open, varied, fluid, and full of possibilities; it enshrines a subversive kind of thought that heralds a transforming of the basis of society and culture. Cixous is notable for an optimism and joy conspicuously lacking in Derrida, with his admission that logocentrism, however deplorable, is after all inevitable. She thinks women can lead a revolt against the dichotomous order of concepts in which we have thus far been immured.[25]

Luce Irigaray is a psychoanalyst who aims to liberate women from masculine philosophies, including those of Derrida and

21. Helene Cixous, "The Laugh of the Medusa," in Elaine Marks and Isabelle de Courtivron, eds., *New French Feminisms* (New York: Schocken Books, 1981), 262.

22. Ibid., 256.

23. Cited by H. V. Wenzel, "The Text as Body/Politics," *Feminist Studies* 7, no. 2 (Summer 1981), 270–71.

24. Marks and Courtivron, *Feminisms,* "Introduction III," 36.

25. Tong, "Feminism," 217, 224–5.

Jacques Lacan. According to Lacan, a child at the earliest stage of life is the captive of illusory images. Later on the boy, once he passes what Sigmund Freud identified as the "Oedipal" stage,[26] leaves the realm of what Lacan calls the "Imaginary," and becomes liberated by entering the "Symbolic order" of language and selfhood. Girls are said never properly to resolve the conflicts of the Oedipal stage, and so, even when they are mature women, to remain trapped to a greater extent than men in the realm of the Imaginary. Irigaray points out that there may be a positive aspect to this alleged entrapment. Women and their sexuality have been seen too much from a masculine point of view. Is it not desirable to find ways of envisaging and realizing women's possibilities that are not mediated through men? For this purpose, one has to study carefully, but with a very critical eye, those texts in philosophy and psychoanalysis that have envisaged women in relation to men and so belittled them.[27] Still, one must resist any attempt actually to redefine the feminine; this would only reconfirm a basically masculine point of view. "To claim that the feminine can be expressed in the form of a concept is to allow oneself to be caught up again in a system of 'masculine' representations, in which women are trapped in a system or meaning, which serves the auto-affection of the (masculine) subject."[28]

Masculine thought, as Irigaray sees it, has never been able to understand woman as anything other than a reflection of man. Typical of this prejudice is the thinking of Freud, who saw woman as not so much *different* as *lacking*—lacking a penis.

26. I.e., that of rivalry with the parent of the same sex for possession of the parent of the opposite sex. The reference is to the Greek mythical figure Oedipus, who inadvertently killed his father and married his mother.

27. Cf. Claire Duchen, *Feminism in France* (London: Routledge and Kegan Paul, 1986), 87–88.

28. Luce Irigaray, *This Sex Which Is Not One* (Ithaca, N.Y.: Cornell University Press, 1985), 32. Tong, "Feminism," 227, 269.

One effective way of releasing the repressed "feminine feminine"—that is, woman as seen and expressing herself from her own point of view and in her own way—is to engage in lesbian and autoerotic practices. Another useful device is mimicry, where one endeavors "to *undo* the effects of phallocentric discourse simply by *overdoing* them."[29] There is throughout Irigaray's work a tension between the desire to stop labelling on the one hand and a recognition on the other that labelling is inevitable. But then, self-contradiction is for her a way of rebelling against phallocentrism with its zeal for consistency. "(S)he (woman) sets off in all directions leaving 'him' (man) unable to discern the coherence of any meaning. Hers are contradictory words, somewhat mad from the standpoint of reason, inaudible for whoever listens to them with ready-made grids, with a fully elaborated code in hand."[30]

Julia Kristeva sets herself against the tendency to identify the "feminine" and the "masculine" with biological women and men. She points out that girls can identify with their fathers, and boys with their mothers; women may write in a "masculine," men in a "feminine" manner. To insist that women write differently from men is to force both sexes back into the constraints imposed on them by patriarchy. In any case, "woman as such does not exist"[31]—the assumption that she does is part and parcel of the essentialist metaphysics that one ought to try to deconstruct. "Woman is a valid concept politically, but not philosophically"; as Kristeva says, "There are still many goals which women can achieve: freedom of abortion and contraception, daycare centers for children, equality on the job, etc. Therefore we must use 'we are women' as an advertisement or

29. Moi, *Politics,* 140.

30. Irigaray, *This Sex,* 29. Tong, "Feminism," 227–29.

31. Julia Kristeva, *About Chinese Women* (New York: Urizen Books, 1974), 1–16.

slogan for our demands. On a deeper level, however, a woman cannot 'be.'"[32] She links the revolution of society to that of language, maintaining that "the historical and political experiences of the twentieth century have demonstrated that one cannot be transformed without the other."[33]

Kristeva thinks the scapegoating of groups to be grounded in what she calls the "abject," the irrational disgust one picks up at the pre-Oedipal stage for aspects of one's own and one's mother's body. A repudiation of the feminine is one aspect of this more general tendency. She insists on the importance of society coming to terms with the "abject," with what it has marginalized and repressed, which is to be found in the discourses associated with irrationality, insanity, and sexuality, all of which are swept under the carpet by phallogocentric thought. Language that is "rational," "objective," and normal in its grammar and syntax is redolent of repression. To break through such repression we need a writing that emphasizes sound and color and is marked by grammatical and syntactical dislocations—this will enable us to confront and assimilate what disgusts or horrifies us. The point is not to rid ourselves of all that is objective or rational or post-Oedipal, but effectively to acknowedge the interplay of the two sides of our nature, of its order and disorder.[34]

Postmodern feminists are often criticized for the fact that rather than engaging in sit-ins, protest marches, and so on, they write in an elitist manner, which few but themselves can understand, from a cushioned academic environment.[35] This criti-

32. From an interview with *Tel Quel;* in Marks and Courtivron, *Feminisms,* 157.

33. Kristeva, *Revolution in Poetic Languages* (New York: Columbia University Press, 1984).

34. See "The Novel as Polylogue," in Kristeva, *Desire in Language* (New York: Columbia University Press, 1982), 159–209.

35. For this and other criticisms, see Tong, "Feminism," 231–32.

cism is in itself hardly to be taken seriously. It would obviously be absurd to run down, say, pharmacologists in favor of hospital doctors; unless the pharmacologists did their research in an academic environment that ensured the utmost objectivity, and unless they availed themselves of a technical language that would be daunting to any layperson, the doctors, with the best will in the world, would not be able to cure patients so effectively and would be rather more liable than they are at present to kill them or at least make their ailments worse. Similarly, any serious movement of social reform needs theorists sufficiently detached from the immediate struggle to think about the direction in which the movement is going, and the good to be achieved and the evils to be remedied and avoided by it. And, for all the dangers incurred of forming "superior" little cliques protected by sententious but obfuscating jargon, such theorists are likely to need a technical language if their analysis of what is to be done, and how it is to be done, is to be anything other than superficial. In any case, it is not too difficult for a sympathetic and moderately educated reader to get the hang of what postmodern feminism is about.

As to the espousal by postmodern feminists of the particular theories promulgated by Freud and Lacan, it may be thought to be a pity that they base arguments essential to their position on ideas that are themselves so controversial.[36] But I think the following points should be conceded: that the development of our emotional and intellectual life depends crucially on our early environment and upbringing, and particularly on our relations with our parents and other caregivers; that reason and objectivity arrive comparatively late on the scene; and that our special modern preoccupation with reason and objectivity, which indeed is necessitated by modern technology, creates a

36. On the insights and oversights of Freudian theory, see Meynell, *Freud, Marx and Morals* (New York: Barnes and Noble, 1981), chap. 5.

special problem about achieving a tolerable relation to our emotions and feelings. Also sexual stereotyping, and bias about the supposed superiority of one sex to the other, may make it difficult or impossible for individuals to find fulfilment and to contribute to the good of the community to the extent that they might otherwise do.

There is no doubt that, as Freud emphasized, rationality is a burden and leaves us with a painful hankering after an existence more in tune with our instincts. Yet he stressed that we are all the same better off for our possession and use of reason.[37] Freud's view of the prospects for a more comfortable coexistence of reason and instinct is perhaps excessively bleak; yet surely he had a point. We need a critical consciousness, whether we are women or men, if our lives are not to be (in Thomas Hobbes's famous phrase) nasty, brutish, and short. We long for the more spontaneous instinctual life, and how to achieve a tolerable balance here is a perennial problem. The positive side of postmodern feminism, as represented perhaps most effectively by Kristeva, urges us to look for a more satisfactory balance than we have at present. The negative side, which I find especially in Irigaray, invites us to abjure critical consciousess, to go with the flow of our instincts—which will consign us all to the devil in short order. Freud also pointed out that a thoroughgoing rationality would take instinct into account and not make demands on it which it is incapable of fulfilling.[38] One should not mistake the inadequate and incomplete rationality that has sometimes afflicted the Old Enlightenment—and which I think may indeed be especially characteristic of the male of our species—for rationality itself. And surely, to glorify women for

37. See especially S. Freud, *Civilization and Its Discontents* (London: Hogarth Press, 1930).

38. See Freud, *New Introductory Lectures on Psychoanalysis, Collected Works* (New York: Norton, 1990), 170–72; cf. Meynell, *Freud,* 132–34.

not being rational, for not being concerned with the precision and exactitude necessary for science and technology, is to play into the hands of those antifeminists who have always harped on the irrationality of women. Worse, it is to sell short the many women who, especially in recent times, have made outstanding contributions to science and philosophy as traditionally understood. The principle of noncontradiction, with all the "binary oppositions" of true and false, right and wrong, in which it issues, is an inalienable part of this rationality. The technologists who, with prodigious nerve, patience and skill, got the Apollo 13 astronauts back to earth against all odds, did not achieve what they did by violating this principle or castigating it as phallologocentric.

I am inclined to think that the balance between reason and instinct may well be somewhat different in the average woman from what it is in the average man, but that any male advantages that may accrue from this are at least balanced by male absurdities. It seems reasonable to suppose that such differences are up to a point written into our biology, since unless women were on the whole strongly programmed by instinct to care for the children that they bear, the human race would not survive. But this by no means implies, as Julia Kristeva does well to remind us, that there are not some women who in character and temperament are just about as "masculine" as any man, and some men who are similarly as "feminine" as almost any woman.

From a New Enlightenment perspective, the trouble is not with conceptualization and systematic reasoning as such, or even with "binary oppositions" when used with common sense and discrimination, but with a conceptual apparatus applied without constant testing and modification in the light of experience. A "scientific" attitude with less rigidity and dogmatism than is sometimes associated with it—when it is blighted by what William Blake called "a confident insolence sprouting from systematic reasoning"—is certainly desirable; and this could well be a good to which women are specially fitted by innate temperament to make a contribution. As to "labelling," the lesson to be learned from a New Enlightenment perspective is not that we should altogether avoid affixing labels, but that we should be on the lookout for the constriction of ourselves and others by such labels, and recognize the capacity that people have for change. Some labels actually tend to open up possibilities of freedom and self-realization. One may take the example of a violent criminal who, due to a course taken in prison, becomes competent to label himself as a skilled calligrapher. But the limitations suggested by labels may have their uses too. Certainly it is true that if you are biologically a woman, and there are patterns of behavior that suit most such persons, they may not happen to suit your particular constitution; but it is probably wise to bear them in mind in case they do.[39]

The notion that women are specially qualified to be agents of revolution seems to me rather questionable. Up to now, I think, they have tended to be a rather conservative force in society, even if Camille Paglia exaggerates when she claims that, if the development of culture had been left in the hands of women, we would all still be living in grass huts.[40] And conservatism, for all its liability to abuse, is by no means to be rejected root and branch, assuming there is anything worth preserving in the civilization that we have inherited. Further, one could argue that the more hare-brained revolutionary proposals are a sort of folly that women should be glad to consign mainly to men. Few women could ever have been so silly as to take seriously Plato's suggestion in the *Republic* about the abolition of

39. According to Donald Symons, the best-known of those women who, in the nineteen-sixties, adopted a style of sexual behavior that has been traditionally associated with males; almost all showed signs of regretting it some years later. See Symons, *The Evolution of Human Sexuality* (Oxford: Oxford University Press, 1979), 220.

40. Camille Paglia, *Sexual Personae* (New York: Random House, 1991), 38.

families.[41] We need particular, special, and lasting bonds of affection to become fully human beings. It happens that, thus far at least, women have made a much greater contribution to the meeting of this need. Probably the unduly detached intellect that comes out with insanely impractical suggestions like Plato's is a typically male phenomenon; yet a measure of detachment is absolutely needed. For example, when it comes to a serious quarrel between two children who are members of different families, the parents of each will, inevitably and quite properly, be predisposed in favor of their own child. But all the same, if justice is to be done, the point of view of the other child must be taken into account in a way that goes against the spontaneous impulses of care for one's own.[42] And when the relation of human groups is in question, tribal or quasi-tribal loyalties are a vital component of human life; we cannot do without them, and should not even wish to do so. But when the question arises of justice between tribes, we have to shoulder the burden of greater moral abstraction.

Irigaray's demand for the "feminine feminine" needs to be generalized; each sex should try to see both itself and the other from the other's point of view. Men can feel powerless too; it is not all jam to face death or dismemberment on the battlefield, or even to be locked into dangerous or alienating work due to

41. *Republic* V 457b–e.

42. The ethic of "care" is often contrasted with the ethic of "justice." I think that this is a serious mistake. The truth of the matter, I believe, is that the "care" which characterizes close human relationships is one of the very greatest goods with the proper distribution of which justice has to be concerned. A vast number of people do not get their share of care; they are thereby made incapable of either being happy themselves or allowing those within their sphere of influence to be happy. Perhaps when there is a conflict between care and justice, women are more inclined to react in favor of care, men of justice; that may be what Freud was getting at when he claimed that women had on average less of a sense of justice than men (*New Lectures*, 129, 134–35). A person who is neither object nor subject of relations of care, so far from being capable of greater justice, is both pitiable and dangerous.

the necessity of supporting a family.[43] The notion that women's point of view on women and men has been largely suppressed needs examination, perhaps, in the light of the fact that so many of the world's greatest novelists (Jane Austen, Charlotte and Emily Bronte, George Eliot) have been women; and that both producers and consumers of that abundantly flourishing genre, the romantic novelette, are almost entirely women.

In their sexualizing of the not-obviously sexual characteristics of women and men, it seems to me that some post-modern feminists, Irigaray in particular, have been unduly influenced by the least helpful aspect of Freud's speculations.[44] Thus the comparison of the pen wielded by the male to his penis is more entertaining than productive of insight. However, when all is said and done, so far as Rosemarie Tong is right in her suggestion, that the main thrust of postmodern feminism is to empower every woman to become herself,[45] such feminism is on balance a real good in New Enlightenment terms. The New Enlightenment ideal is that every human being, female and male, should be freed as far as possible to be able to find fulfilment for herself or himself and contribute to the fulfilment of others. Certainly it is true that women have in some respects been expected to foster the fulfilment of others at the expense of their own. To what extent such great sacrifices are also demanded of men in other respects is moot. If some feminists are inclined to sweep this suggestion aside, one can only comment that, while men's self-satisfaction, smugness, and pretension are always worth a tilt, women do not commend themselves by imitating them.

43. See Warren Farrell, *The Myth of Male Power* (New York: Simon and Schuster, 1993).

44. For the reasons why Freud was driven to his sexual theory, and why it is misleading, see Meynell, *Freud*, 156–57. Sexuality, however important, is only one among several basic components of our instinctual life.

45. Tong, "Feminism," 217.

It is suggested in some quarters that postmodernism need not have the implications attributed to it by either its opponents or some of its extremist advocates. In reference to the dispute between Plato and the Sophists, with which that between modernists and postmodernists has so often rightly been compared, David Kolb will have it that each alternative—the absolutely firm ground of reason and the perpetually shifting sands of the kind of opinion that is swayed by rhetoric—is as flawed as the other. He adds that neither reason nor rhetorical persuasion is a pure power, beyond space and time, that can be applied at will against totally yielding and passive opinions. Actual persuasion is applied, successfully or unsuccessfully, to persons who have definite projects in particular historical situations, which enable them to deal more or less effectively with such situations.[46] However, in spite of what is implied by Kolb, Plato's main concern is not with the mere stability or instability of opinions as such, but rather with whether any ground can be articulated on which one may even approach toward knowledge of what is really true or good. A firmly maintained false opinion or evil disposition, to him, would presumably be at least as much to be avoided as an evanescent or capricious one.[47] If no rational basis can be articulated on which one belief or attitude is really to be preferred to another, as more likely to be true or good, then all beliefs and attitudes must be in the last resort equally arbitrary. Thus the middle ground advocated by Kolb, between a well-founded reason, which tends to get at the real truth about things, and mere persuasion, which can have no such claim or issue, turns out to be illusory.

46. Kolb, *Postmodern Sophistications* (Chicago and London: University of Chicago Press, 1990), 32–33. I find Kolb's argument at this point both confusing and confused; I have produced the best summary of it that I can.

47. It is true that in the *Meno* (98a) Plato contrasts, and in my view quite rightly, the relative stability of well-founded knowledge as compared with ill-founded opinion. But this is not the main point at issue for him.

Kolb maintains that we can have criticism without self-transparency, and that the contrast with total self-opacity implicit in the notion of self-transparency is itself misleading.[48] Even if we cannot conceive of a totally decontextualized self, he says, this does not imply that we cannot recognize possible alternative ways of speaking and acting.[49] But the real question is whether we can have any ground for recognizing one of any pair of such alternatives as liable to be really better, or really closer to the truth, than the other. Further, does the specification of such grounds not presuppose a potential self-transparency of human beings as self-transcendent in the sense for which I have already argued, and so as possessing norms by means of which what is true may in principle be known, and what is good known and implemented? Certainly, total self-transparency is impossible, in that self-knowledge is a continual task for us that is never complete. Kolb will have us cultivate a "disciplined perception";[50] but one wonders what could be the use of such a commodity, except as a means to discerning what is really true or good. Moreover, the falsity of the flat-earth theory is not merely a matter of a particular point of view; nor is the badness of slavery, foot-binding, or torture for the sake of amusement. Persons or whole communities may confidently believe that the earth is flat and that it is proper to own slaves, but this is not the point. And criticism that does not implicitly invoke some absolute standard of rationality and is not aimed to determine what is really true or good, is criticism only in name.

Typically modern, in Kolb's view, is the assumption that we can distinguish sharply between the three worlds of the objective, the subjective, and the social. But this is to underestimate, as he sees it, the degree to which we are immersed in our history.[51] It appears to me, however, that something like what Kolb

48. Kolb, *Sophistications,* 52–53.
49. Ibid., 55.
50. Ibid., 58.
51. Ibid., 63, 72.

calls the "three-world story" is a corollary of the cognitive and moral transcendence for which I have already argued. However much we are immersed in our history, we cannot be so to a degree that renders self-transcendence impossible, and if we were, we would be in no position to assert that we were. As individuals, we have our own feelings, sensations, beliefs, and attitudes, which may be said to make up our subjective worlds. Most of our beliefs and attitudes are shared with other members of our societies and so may be held to make up a social world. The beliefs in question, whether individual or social, tend to be true of the objective world so far as we are unrestrictedly rational in the sense given in the second chapter. (In this sense, the subjective and social worlds are part of the objective world, since we can find out about them by being rational. By this means, I can get to know not only the migratory habits of eagles, but also what blacks in Atlanta think about the American civil war, or how the child at the bottom of the class feels about school.) We are certainly "immersed in history" so far as the evidence to which we are liable to attend, the hypotheses we are able to envisage, and the judgments we are apt to arrive at are enormously affected by the place, time, and circumstances in which we live. Yet we can "transcend" our historical situation so far as at least sometimes to judge what is the case, and indeed what is good, independently of that situation. That Abraham Lincoln was killed by gunshot, and that the practice of *suttee* was bad, in no way depends on my historical situation; and yet I can know that he was killed, and that *suttee* was a bad custom, on the basis of evidence available to me within that situation.

However subtle the palliatives and compromises offered by Kolb and others,[52] the forms of postmodernism that carry the most conviction are the more consistent and radical. In this

52. A rather similar position appears to be held by Richard Bernstein; see his *Beyond Objectivism and Relativism* (Oxford: Blackwells, 1983), xiv, 8, 11, etc.

vein it is said that postmodernism runs constantly at the edge of delirium and doom, and is characterized by "suicidal nihilism . . . nauseous malaise . . . " and the "sickening depair of vertigo."[53] An important influence on the more extreme forms of postmodernism, in both philosophy and the arts, is the work of Georges Bataille. Habermas has remarked that French postmodernism moved toward self-destruction when it followed Bataille. It is fair to say, however, that Bataille is at one with critical theory in his regrets about the absence of the sacred from modern society and his blaming of this absence on the predominance of instrumental reason and the oppressive homogeneity this imposes.[54] Bataille attacks the main currents of modernist thought by advising a return to Nietzsche, and recommends an overcoming of the self in laughter, ecstasy, and death. Bataille exults in the consequences of the "death of God" proclaimed by Nietzsche. In Foucault's words, he "was perfectly conscious of the possibilities of thought that could be released by this death." One kills God for the purposes of ecstasy, "to liberate life from this existence that limits it . . . ; to lose language in a deafening night. The death of God does not restore us to a limited and positivistic world, but to a world exposed by the experience of its limits, made and unmade by the excess which transgresses it."[55] As Bataille sees it (to quote Annette Michelson), it is "in the festivity of sacrifice and in its sacred violence that man attains that community in sovereignty which is lost in the social order founded on the primacy of production and

53. *The Postmodern Scene. Excremental Culture and Hyper-Aesthetics,* by Arthur Kroker and David Cook (Montreal: New World Perspectives, 1986), 11–12. The last two of these choice phrases are due to Georges Bataille, *Visions of Excess. Selected Writings 1927–39* (Minneapolis: University of Minnesota Press, 1985), 84.

54. Cf. Annette Michelson, "Heterology and the Critique of Instrumental Reason," *October* (Spring 1986), 125–26.

55. M. Foucault, *Language, Counter-Memory, Practice* (Ithaca, N.Y.: Cornell University Press, 1977), 32.

acquisition."[56] One is hardly surprised, at this rate, that Bataille felt much in common with the Aztecs, or that his pornography is reputed by aficionados to be some of the finest composed in the course of the present century. It would be understandable, but quite wrong, to infer that Bataille is opposed to all restrictions or taboos. On the contrary, he finds them essential to the reality of transgression. It is only by means of transgression that the sacred and ecstatic can enter the profane and secular world.[57] (One is reminded of St. Augustine's recollection, in the *Confessions,* of his boyhood escapade of stealing pears; what bothered him most in retrospect was that the fun depended so largely on the knowledge that he was doing something wrong.)[58]

Julian Pefanis pertinently asks whether one is to take Bataille seriously, and if so, how.[59] The right, if somewhat disappointing, answer to this question is that Bataille, like so many writers of postmodernist tendency, supplies an important corrective to some features of modern culture, but in a grossly exaggerated form. How can we balance production and consumption with other means for realizing the human good, reconciling them as well with the need for preserving a world that is a fit habitation for the human soul as well as the human body? We need passion and ecstasy, as well as the sobriety that is necessary for sheer survival and the preservation of tolerable relations with other persons and human groups, and with the rest of nature.

Mention of the death of God brings us to the matter alluded to very briefly at the end of the second chapter—something that amounts to the skeleton in the closet of the New Enlightenment. Many people, following the trail blazed by the French leaders of the Old Enlightenment, have regarded the advance

56. Michelson, "Critique," 116.

57. Pefanis, *Heterology,* 40, 44–46, 49–50, 54, 137–38.

58. Augustine, *Confessions,* II, 16; E. B. Pusey's translation (London: J. M. Dent, 1907), 30.

59. Ibid., 57.

of the human intellect, in unravelling the secrets of the universe including human nature, as issuing in a scientific materialism which implies atheism and a rejection of religion. Nietzsche and Derrida, on the other hand, have descried a close connection between belief in a God on the one hand, and confidence that the universe will yield its secrets to the human intellect on the other. The following argument, which is valid in the technical sense that its conclusions follow ineluctably from its premisses, will bear thinking about in this connection:

> If the world is amenable to intellectual inquiry, there must be something analogous to intelligence at the bottom of it.
>
> But the world is amenable to intellectual inquiry.
>
> Therefore there must be something analogous to intelligence at the bottom of it.

The atheist heirs of the Old Enlightenment assume the truth of the second (minor) premiss as a matter of course, for all that they do not usually make it explicit; they avoid the conclusion by rejecting the first (major) premiss. It is curious that Nietzsche, Bataille, and Derrida, along with many postmodernist authors, appear to accept the major premiss and avoid the conclusion by rejecting the minor—the world is not really intelligible, as science might make it appear to be, but its apparent intelligibility is due to the imposition upon it of the categories of the human understanding. I have argued elsewhere that this is not really a defensible view, presupposing as it does either that reality is directly apprehended in experience (in which case it reduces to subjectivity) or that it is not really apprehended by us at all (as in Kant's doctrine of the inaccessibility of "things in themselves").[60] The principles of the New Enlightenment seem to require that one accept both premisses and conclusion

60. See Hugo Meynell, *The Intelligible Universe* (New York: Barnes and Noble, 1982).

of the above argument, and so are apt to lead to some kind of theism.

Still, the religion that usually issues from or presupposes theism comes in many shapes and sizes. Of the greatest importance for the New Enlightenment, perhaps, is the contrast between the sort of theism where the effect of the command of God is ultimately to enhance our nature (however arduous the discipline required to do this) and the sort where, in both the short and the long run, it in fact, even if not in theory, thwarts or diminishes it. Both Old and New Enlightenment are vehemently opposed to the second of these attitudes associated with theism, where theistic religion seems to act as a pretext for the tyranny over some human beings by others who combine a taste for the exercise of power with a deep-seated hatred of human fulfilment or self-realization. In no area of human concern is this phenomenon so conspicuous as in that of sexuality. Perhaps the tension between our need to keep constraints on our raw impulses, and the equally imperative need to keep a sufficiently keen edge on our zest for the immediate business of living, is most palpable here. Foucault's work on the history of human efforts to cope with the problem are of great value, if only one can keep clearly in mind the question that never seems to come properly into focus in his work—how can human desires and impulses be coordinated in such a way that happiness is realized as far as possible without the sacrifice of fairness? The combined folly, ineffectiveness, and cruelty of many traditional attitudes to human sexuality, as described by Foucault and others, really beggar description, and will surely astonish our descendants, assuming that we have any.[61]

61. See G. R. Taylor, *Sex in History* (London: Thames and Hudson, 1954).

6

GIFT FOR THE GHOST

ON DERRIDA'S REPUTATION

MANY PEOPLE are unable to make up their minds as to whether Jacques Derrida's work is "one of the most stunning adventures of modern thought,"[1] or whether it is rather the *ultima Thule* of the higher hogwash. Christoper Norris, in a very critical survey of postmodernism, singles out Derrida as one whose philosophical rigor shows that he is not to be classed with the usual run of postmodernists.[2] A rather different view was expressed in a letter to the London *Times* of May 9th, 1992. This was signed by a group of professional philosophers, all of them eminent, from a number of countries and institutions. It suggested that Derrida was not a suitable candidate for the award of an honorary degree by Cambridge University, on the grounds that, though describing himself as a philosopher, he produced work that did not seem to other philosophers to "meet . . . standards of clarity and rigour" such as are generally

1. Peggy Kamuf, "Preface" to *A Derrida Reader. Between the Blinds* (New York: Columbia University Press, 1991), vii.

2. C. Norris, *The Truth About Postmodernism* (Oxford: Blackwell, 1993), 93, 27–28, 300–303.

expected within the discipline.[3] Derrida's adversaries acknowledge that he has considerable talent of a sort; what they deny is that his talent is of a sort proper to those who would call themselves philosophers.

Derrida has published a lengthy response to the letter. It is worth meeting his demands, demands which he says his adversaries have not met,[4] to the extent of citing it in detail. The new powers available to academics through the media, he complains, tempt them to throw over the restraints imposed on them within the university and to bring pressure to bear through the press and public opinion on ways of thinking of which they happen to disapprove. As a consequence, "our responsibility is to redefine rules, to invent others (for journalists as well as for academics), a huge and formidable task" and indeed an endless one.[5] The need for this is abundantly shown by the letter, in which the signatories claim that their concern is to protect Cambridge University and universities in general. But they do so by means of generalized and rabble-rousing slogans rather than by careful argument and detailed citation of particular texts. One may indeed wonder whether there has ever been a worse offense against the principle of academic freedom. Just suppose that the State, or some other powerful institution, had attempted to exert power in this way on those who wanted to award Derrida an honorary degree, "calling in question their ability to decide for themselves in intellectual matters"! Derrida's sponsors were treated with contempt and subjected to "advice such as one would bestow on children or illiterates." How his adversaries must have felt threatened, thus to lose their self-control![6]

In fact, this "international militia" betrays the very principles it purports to defend, and that in several ways.[7] The phrase

3. Jacques Derrida, *Points . . . Interviews, 1974–1994* (Stanford, Calif.: Stanford University Press, 1995), 419–20.

4. Ibid., 406.

5. Ibid., 402.

6. Ibid., 403.

7. Ibid., 403–4.

"logical phalluses" that it attributes to Derrida in fact occurs nowhere in his writings. His adversaries appear to think that "the influence of philosophy on other disciplines or more generally outside the profession" implies that "it can't be philosophy"; and they use the Press "to put about the idea that philosophy . . . should not be open to the judgment of scholars of other disciplines!" However, philosophy at its best has never permitted itself to be confined within such limits. Furthermore, his adversaries complain that his writing "defies comprehension," while at the same time "denouncing its excessive influence"; they "end up by saying that there is nothing to understand" in Derrida's work "except the false and the trivial."[8]

The whole episode of their intervention is of course extremely funny; but this by no means prevents it from being serious as well. We must be open to both aspects in such cases, and "never give up either the laughter or the seriousness of intellectual and ethico-political responsibility."[9] The academics concerned purport to speak in the name of "reason, truth and scholarship," but every sentence of their letter constitutes a violation of these ideals.[10] Yet for all their "anxious obscurantism," they still exercise a formidable power, given that they can use for their own ends the international distribution and prestige of such a paper as the London *Times*. Against such abuse of power, unfortunately, "a discourse which is argued through, which is slow, difficult, rigorous, will have but little purchase."[11]

Sarah Richmond, another academic, has called Derrida's work "poison for young people," and *Der Spiegel* has seen fit to echo her abuse in the title of an article, "Poison for the Spirit." Here we have an alliance of journalists using their formidable powers of publicity, with academics "who say whatever they like, with no proof and no discussion." Roger Scruton, again, is

8. Ibid., 404.
9. Ibid.
10. Ibid., 404–5.
11. Ibid., 405.

quoted by the same weekly to the effect that Derrida's thinking amounts to "pure nihilism"; he has made similar remarks in the Press for a number of years.[12] If Scruton really thinks that Derrida is a nihilist, he should "at least begin to find out a little more about my work." As far as he is concerned, apparently it is "in vain that I have been protesting for thirty years against nihilism." If Scruton insists "that what I say, literally, quite explicitly, page after page, in favor of a way of thinking which is affirmative and not nihilist is not convincing," he ought to make particular citations to substantiate such damaging charges. Travesties of this kind can come only from academics and journalists who have not "read, properly read, one line of my books."[13]

I have always deplored the conventional prejudice of "Anglo-Saxons" against "Continental" philosophers, and have found a great deal to admire in the work of Nietzsche, Husserl, Heidegger, Sartre, and even Foucault. So when I first started attending to Derrida's work I was by no means predisposed against him. But the fact remains that, after reading substantial amounts of material written by Derrida, and on him by persons who are favorably impressed by his work, I can find no reason to disagree with the signatories of the above-mentioned letter, which summed up with extraordinary brevity and clarity, and with considerable wit, conclusions to which I had come more or less tentatively myself.

There was nothing in the letter to imply that the authorities at Cambridge who wanted to give Derrida an honorary degree were like children or illiterates. Presumably the finest academic institutions can make mistakes—for example, in honoring someone whose work turns out to be worthless, or who is ultimately to be revealed as a fraud, cheat, or plagiarist. And it is surely not merely the right, but the duty, of qualified persons

12. Ibid. 13. Ibid., 406.

who are concerned with the overall quality of intellectual life, to warn them when they think that there is a real danger of such mistakes being made. Admittedly, steps of this kind should not be taken without weighty reasons, and they ought to be pondered with the utmost care; but they are not be ruled out as inappropriate in principle. I am afraid I have so far seen nothing in Derrida's work, least of all in his *apologia* in reply to the letter, to convince me that the steps were inappropriate in this case. They were certainly not opposing Derrida's freedom of speech, or anyone else's; the signatories to the letter were exercising their own right to freedom of speech, and indeed fulfilling their duty to do so if they thought, after careful deliberation, that it was for the common good. They may have been sincerely mistaken in thinking so, but that is hardly to the point; and in any case, in my view they were not so mistaken.[14]

Those who are of two minds about Derrida's credentials as a philosopher may care to consider his account of Plato's suggestions in the *Phaedrus* about the merits and possible defects of writing as a supplement to speech.[15] The little fable told by Socrates makes the point that though writing is in many ways obviously a great good, it is perhaps not an unmixed good. Writing is clearly an invaluable aid to knowledge and memory.

14. In point of fact, I believe that there are a few important philosophical points to be unearthed from Derrida's writings: (1) His aspersions on the mistaken view that we can refer more directly to the contents of our consciousness than to the things and events of the external world (this is interestingly related to Ludwig Wittgenstein's polemic against the notion of a "private language" in the *Philosophical Investigations* [Oxford: Blackwell, 1958], paras. 243–317); (2) His early argument against Foucault that one has to presuppose reason in arguing against reason; (3) His bringing out of how the individual subject is as much dominated by language as capable of exercising power over or through it. But these points are so overlaid by distractions and irrelevancies as to be quite difficult to recover from his work as a whole, which seems to me well described by the letter to the *Times*.

15. Plato, *Phaedrus*, 274b–278e. Cf. A. E. Taylor, *Plato. The Man and His Work* (London: Methuen, 1960), 316–17.

On the other hand, once writing prevails, oral memory declines. Also, if I am trying to explain something to an audience, I can modify my expression according to the audience's understanding of the topic, whereas what is written is down once and for all in a way that does not take into account the particular viewpoint of each reader. Derrida compares this to Freud's famous example, of the man accused of ruining the kettle that he had borrowed. The man replies that he never borrowed the kettle in the first place, that it was full of holes when he borrowed it, that it was in the same brand new state when he gave it back as when he got it, and so on.[16] The general point to be borne in mind here is that qualification is not, except in certain circumstances, contradiction. If I say that a man is even-tempered, but that once in his life he shouted at his wife for some trivial reason, I am not contradicting myself. On the other hand, if I say that he is even-tempered, yet at the same time frequently flies off the handle with or without the slightest provocation, then this is at least at first sight a contradiction. (I say "at first sight," to forestall the objection that one can no doubt think up elaborate stories of situations in which this might seem the right thing to say.) Again, if I commend a concert pianist as a magnificent performer, but admit that one evening she gave an indifferent performance of K 503, when distracted by news of her father-in-law's arrest for soliciting, I am not contradicting myself. But I am doing so, to all intents and purposes, if I say she is an excellent concert pianist, but never performs any piece in which she does not make at least three egregious errors in the first five bars. There is not the slightest indication that the qualifications to the thesis about the usefulness of writing ascribable to Plato in the *Phaedrus* amount to contradictions; and if they do not, Derrida's objections simply fall to the ground.[17]

16. "Plato's Pharmacy"; see Kamuf, *Reader,* 135–36.

17. The same applies, so far as I can see, to practically everything that Derrida says on the subject of "supplements."

One can write philosophy, or one can write somewhat dizzily exuberant *belles lettres* with philosophy as pretext. The latter sort of writing, which seems to me the one that Derrida has made his own, may be all very well, but it is not philosophy, and it is definitely not useful for the important tasks that face philosophy, of dispelling conceptual confusions, and of clarifying our apprehension of what is true and what is good. Derrida's *Glas*[18] starts *in medias res,* as though one had turned a page, in the middle of a sentence—or rather in the middle of two sentences, those of the juxtaposed Hegel and Genet commentaries. What is the point of starting in this fashion, or of the juxtaposition itself? Does either commentary throw any light on the other? Was it meant to? What is the point of all the different sizes of print? Is not the point perhaps, as Bernard Lonergan used to say, that there is no point?

I believe that the central principle underlying Derrida's work can be expressed in Coleridgean terms—it is perhaps the best example extant of "fancy" masquerading as "imagination."[19]

18. Lincoln, Neb.: University of Nebraska Press, 1986.

19. S. T. Coleridge, *Biographia Literaria*, at the end of Chapter XIII (London: J. M. Dent 1956), 167. In the following passage, the editorial explanations, added in square brackets, make it unusually clear what is going on. "The end of enjoyment is the end of enjoyment: the final point, period. The bone or snag [*L' os:* in German, the lot, *Los;* in Latin, the mouth, *os*] of enjoyment, the chance and its loss, is that enjoyment must sacrifice itself in order to be there, in order to give itself its there, in order to touch, and tamper with, its *Da-sein.* [The] *telos* [tel os: such *os*] of enjoyment equals death—that would be the end point (the point-of-no-end-at-all) if there were not, for the untiring desire of speculative dialectics, yet one more turn, annuli yet to be accomplished, and anniversaries to be celebrated" (Derrida, *Glas,* trans. J. P. Leavey and R. Rand [Lincoln, Neb., and London: University of Nebraska Press, 1986], 260). *The Post Card. From Socrates to Freud and Beyond*, trans. Alan Bass (Chicago and London: University of Chicago Press, 1987) makes amusing play with a postcard that reproduces a curious picture by a medieval artist. This represents "Socrates" and "plato" [sic], but evidently gets them mixed up, as "Socrates" is writing, and "plato" is standing just behind him. Having exclaimed about the mistake (9), Derrida drags in a singularly far-fetched sexual interpretation (18), and talks of raving about or delivering the card (delire,

"Fancy" is a matter of breaking up customary patterns of association in a random way. A famous example is the Walrus's proposal of suitable topics of conversation in Lewis Carroll's *Through the Looking-Glass*—"shoes and ships and sealing-wax, . . . cabbages and kings, . . . why the sea is boiling hot, and whether pigs have wings." Imagination creates or envisages a new unity; what is apparently random suddenly hangs together in an unexpected unity, as in the successful interpretation of a heap of clues by a detective, a great work of art, or a newly discovered scientific theory. For the greatest artists and scientists, fancy has certainly been an important means to shake the mind out of its habitual prejudices, assumptions, and associations. But imagination is always the end, the envisagement of the new unity, hypothesis, or viewpont. Feats of sheer fancy

---

delivre) (21). "S" and "p" put him in mind of a predicate contained in a subject (33), and of an equation with two unknowns; which in turn brings in a reference to Freud's introduction of a second unknown in *Beyond the Pleasure Principle.* Freud, in dealing with Greek philosophy, had to take account of the time that had elapsed between himself and the early Greeks; which inspires Derrida to construct a quite hilarious picture of Freud trying to telephone his predecessors from America to Europe, getting into a tizzy because he hasn't got enough change, and perplexed by the time difference (decalage horaire) (31). It can be instructive to analyze out the contents of the witch's brew, and one can admire the skill with which Derrida mixes them up, his *ars combinatoria* (I would hate to essay a Derridean commentary on *that*). A translator's note to *The Post Card* tells us, of the sentence CE-N'EST-PAS-DU-TOUT-UNE-TRANCHE (503): "This sentence plays on lexical and syntactic undecidability. Une tranche is the usual French word for a slice, as in a slice of cake, from the verb *trancher,* to slice. In French psychoanalytic slang, *une tranche* is also the period of time one spends with a given analyst . . . Further, the expression *du tout* can mean either 'of the whole' or 'at all.' Thus, the sentence can mean 'This is not a "slice" (a piece, in the analytic sense or not) of the whole,' or 'This is not at all a "slice" ' (in any sense). The verb *trancher* can also mean to decide on a question or to resolve it in a clear-*cut* way; the English 'trenchant' has a similar sense. Throughout this interview the senses of *tranche* and 'trench' beckon toward each other . . ." One can get quite addicted to this kind of play with learned associations, a game at which Derrida is certainly an unrivalled master. Whether it helps one to think usefully about anything at all is moot.

may well pass for the achievements of genuine imagination, especially when there is social power to reinforce their pretensions. You dare not say that you don't get it; you assume that your mentors and superiors have got it; but there is in fact nothing to get. It is this apparent feature of Derrida's writing that accounts for the seeming contradiction he points out in his adversaries' letter: their saying his work defies comprehension, while complaining about its excessive influence.

If the actual phrase "logical phalluses" never turns up anywhere in Derrida's voluminous work, then it was certainly a tactical error on the part of his adversaries to refer to it as typical of him. Yet it is surely a good example of a practice that is to be found over and over again in Derrida's writings, of developing fanciful associations from the words he uses, associations that distract the mind from any argument or assertion of fact that may happen to be at issue. He inveighs against his adversaries for failing to cite concrete examples. So it seems appropriate to draw attention here to his suggestion, in a contribution to a collection on the "States of Theory" (i.e. literary theory), that the state of theory is southern California. One can only quote the pungent comment of Eeyore the donkey: "Amusing in a quiet way, but not really helpful."[20]

There is no doubt that Derrida can be quite entertaining in this vein, but he lacks the mastery in this respect of, say, the late P. G. Wodehouse or Paul Jennings. The latter informs us, in an uproarious fantasy on English place-names, that "Thirsk" means the desire for vodka; and he gets splendid comic effects by translating the word "damit," in a set of German instructions on how to play the board-game of Halma, as "damn it."[21] Verbal

20. See *The House at Pooh Corner,* by A. A. Milne (McClelland and Stewart, 1925), 68.

21. See *The Jenguin Pennings,* by Paul Jennings (Harmondsworth: Penguin Books, 1963).

pyrotechnics of this kind are not only delightful in themselves, but an excellent means of relaxing and invigorating the mind. Indeed, one may well break a mental log-jam or develop a radically new viewpoint by such means. This is the essence of what Edward de Bono advocated under the title of "lateral thinking."[22] On the New Enlightenment view, it is an important aspect of a comprehensive rationality, so far from being something to be contrasted with, let alone opposed to it. To assume that verbal pyrotechnics and rationality are thus opposed is a mistake shared by most important postmodernists, in this agreeing in an interesting way with some representatives of the Old Enlightenment. However, such indulgence of random associations is a menace when treated as equivalent to or a substitute for argument that is supposed to establish or corroborate, undermine or refute, judgments of fact or value on serious subjects. Humankind is not benefited by this sort of distraction from the questions of how we can avert nuclear war, or put off the extermination of cod, or find a cure for AIDS. So far as this is really the effect of Derrida's work—as it would be easy though invidious to show that it is on the work of some of his acolytes—then one can only agree with Sarah Richmond and *Der Spiegel* that it is a sort of poison for the spirit.

Nothing is more characteristic of Derrida's writings than the sort of intellectual game, or rather perhaps intellectual malpractice, that I have just described—if the most obvious meanings of the sentences that he writes are to be trusted. It is possible that a "deeper reading" than one of which I myself am capable would reveal quite a different picture, and I am quite willing to admit myself in the wrong if I can be convinced of this. But I can find no evidence of it except in the mere say-so of Derrida and his followers. If I am right, Derrida is among the most skilful players of all time of the Two Clubs Gambit as described

22. E. de Bono, *Lateral Thinking* (New York: Harper and Row, 1973).

by Stephen Potter.[23] In Potter's example, a man belongs to an arts club and a military club. He stands out among the artists as a typical military man, a tower of strength on whom the tormented psychoneurotics who constitute the rest of the membership can rely for support. But in the military club he is conspicuous as the one sensitive soul, the delicacy of whose emotions his hardbitten companions can only marvel at and sympathize with from a distance. It was said of Lord Balfour that the philosophers tolerated his deficiencies as a philosopher because they thought that he was primarily a statesman, whereas statesmen put up with his blunders in that capacity because they thought that he was really a philosopher. I myself, having for many years been a member both of a Philosophy Department and a Department of Theology and Religious Studies, have played the Two Clubs Gambit in my own small way. I felt that the philosophers kindly overlooked my incompetence as a formal logician because they thought that I was a theologian, and that the theologians were charitable in the matter of my ignorance of Hebrew because they assumed that I was a philosopher.

It may rightly be inferred from this that I do not have any more sympathy than does Derrida for the view that each academic should stick to her last. I am by no means of the opinion that philosophers should confine their attention to strictly philosophical matters, on literary authorities to literature. Indeed, I would maintain that the health of both subjects depends on their practitioners *not* restricting themselves in this way. I can scarcely afford to do otherwise, having over the years been a rather assiduous poacher in intellectual fields over which I can lay no claim to ownership. But if a person makes statements that belong within a specialty and purports to be an expert within it, it is surely to be taken seriously into account if a rather

23. Stephen Potter, *One-upmanship* (New York: Holt, 1955).

large number of recognized practitioners of the specialty, from a wide range of backgrounds and affiliations, believe that both claims are mistaken or fraudulent. Suppose Smith, a professor of biochemistry, makes revolutionary proposals in Egyptology. If a dozen Egyptologists from as many backgrounds say that her proposals are of little or no merit, Smith and her followers ought to think rather carefully before hurling back accusations of prejudice, blindness, or dishonesty. Notoriously, of course, specialists are by no means infallible, even within the limits of their specialty. Smith could still (at a pinch) be right even if all the recognized authorities in the subject agreed that her proposals were absurd. But this is not the point, which is that any rational person will be disposed to take the opinions of such experts carefully into account when assessing Smith's views. It is misleading, though artful, of Derrida, to imply that his adversaries object to any influence by philosophers on academics outside their own specialty. Their point rather was, that if someone who claimed to be a philosopher impressed only those outside the specialty, this would raise some question about her or his credentials as a philosopher.

As to the charge of nihilism and Derrida's response to it, it is not clear to me how what I understand as Derrida's stance differs from what I take to be extreme instance of one kind of nihilism, or at least what leads inevitably to it. The element of hysterical exaggeration in Derrida's response ("page after page" and so on) does not help, here or elsewhere. One wonders why he could not have said something like, "this obviously non-nihilistic position was what I was getting at on page x of Y, when I argued as follows," etc. At least I, in spite of quite extensive reading of Derrida's work, have not found anything like a clear or explicit statement of an anti-nihilist position. What I have apparently found is a series of rhetorical devices and simulacra of argument by means of which any position whatever, whether on a matter of fact or of value, can appear to be demolished or rather, as they say, "sent up." As to the claim that his adversaries have not "really read" him, I suspect that the only criterion that Derrida would accept for anyone's having "really read" his work is that she ends up more favorably disposed to it than myself or the signatories of the letter. It is always possible that a more extensive or more insightful reading of Derrida's work, or of *Mein Kampf,* or of *The Flopsy Bunnies,* will reveal previously unsuspected depths of significance; but life is too short to give everyone the benefit of the doubt. In any case, Derrida has provided his readers with good reason to believe that the question, of what Derrida's real meaning is, is unanswerable and deliberately designed by Derrida to be so. After all, there is at first sight at least (or is this itself due to a merely superficial reading?) a great deal of polemic in his writings against the notion that an unequivocal interpretation is to be had of anything whatever. (What, after all, is "what"? Is *is* "is"?)

On a more favorable interpretation, Derrida's career is a remarkable example of how one of extrardinary talent and originality can leave persons whom one would suppose well-qualified to judge so strongly convinced that he is a charlatan; on a less favorable, it is a source for fascinating insights into the psychology and sociology of reputation. I am told that one distinguished philosopher has suggested that the whole vogue of what is called "deconstruction" is due to a misunderstanding by members of the Yale Department of English of a few jokes cracked by Derrida.

Some have complained that Derrida is guilty of collapsing different genres of writing—in particular philosophy and literature—into one another, but Christopher Norris defends him against the imputation.[24] Norris remarks on the fact that Habermas, one of those making this charge against Derrida, is himself

24. C. Norris, *What Is Wrong with Postmodernism?* (Baltimore: Johns Hopkins University Press, 1991).

singularly lacking in literary grace. But this is beside the point. Whether a judgment in science, philosophy, or the realm of common sense is true or adequately grounded is one thing; whether it is put over in good English, German, or whatever is another. A fine literary style, as is illustrated by philosophers from Plato through Berkeley to Russell and Quine, can add graciousness to the expression of truth and persuasiveness to good argument; it may also on occasion cover up the false or the sophistical. (It is true that good writing *in general* tends to enhance consciousness, and so heads toward true judgment and valid argument; and that turgid or slovenly expression is apt to to benumb or confuse it. But this is a slightly different matter.) For my part, I think that the crucial distinction to be made here is between language that is in the business of directly stating what is the case, and is to be evaluated accordingly, and the kind that is not. Whether Bohemia does or does not have a sea coast is not relevant to the evaluation of Shakespeare's *The Winter's Tale* (which seems to imply that it has one), in a way that it evidently would be to that of a tourists' guide to the area of Europe that once went by that name. Crick and Watson's discovery of the double helix was in fact announced to the scientific community in a piece of admirable English prose, but the discovery would have been just as important however poor the style of the announcement. I have no doubt that Norris is right to the extent that Derrida does not anywhere state unequivocally that there is no real distinction to be made between philosophy and literature; however, this is merely a natural consequence of the fact that Derrida seldom unequivocally states anything.[25] And I have not found anything in his writings to

25. Thus, in spite of his remarks cited in chapter 3, pp. 60–61, 63 above, Derrida can say: "The value of truth (and all those values associated with it) is never contested or destroyed in my writings" ("Afterword" to the second edition of *Limited Inc.* (Evanston, Ill.: Northwestern University Press 1989), 146; cited in Norris, *Postmodernism,* 300.

show that he takes account of the distinction that I have mentioned, or to suggest that it has ever occurred to him that it might be of some importance.

It has been said of Peter Abelard, that he raised the whole level of intellectual life in the Europe of his time. Perhaps a future historian will say of Derrida that he lowered it all over the whole English-speaking intellectual world of the late twentieth century.

"Deconstruction" is associated with the name of Paul de Man as well as that of Derrida. The two men also have in common that they are singled out by Christopher Norris as thinkers too profound to be classed with the common run of postmodernists. This is not the place to go deep into the notorious obscurities of de Man's writings, but there are points to be made in regard to them which are relevant to our purposes here.

De Man, especially in his later work (from about the middle of the nineteen-sixties onwards), is strongly opposed to the "mystical organicist" outlook on nature purveyed by the romanticism of the late eighteenth and early nineteenth centuries. There is no doubt that this way of looking at things can be abused. Nazi "thinking with the blood" is probably the most notorious instance.[26] It may have the effect of confusing and inhibiting rationality, thus affecting for the worse our capacity to apprehend what is really true and good. But, from a New Enlightenment perspective at least, it also has a positive use, in encouraging and enhancing this capacity. Something like the "mystical-organicist" view may also express and assist in the mind's delighted contemplation of nature as something connatural to it, in opposition to the spiritually arid instrumentalism

26. See Norris, *Postmodernism,* 129–30. I suppose this is what Derrida means, when he claims that de Man's later work in some way makes up for his earlier activities; see pp. 95–96 above.

that sees nature as merely to be controlled and plundered, and is one of the worst legacies of modernity. It may also be noted that the mystical streak so prominent in the writings of many twentieth-century physicists is allied to this side of romanticism.[27]

De Man's admirers have stressed his "epistemological" as opposed to "rhetorical" preoccupations. I am not aware of anywhere in his writings where he clearly sets out satisfactory epistemological principles. Short of such principles, it seems impossible to get a clear idea of the nature of "ideology" in the abusive sense, such ideology being after all a matter of failure to use properly the mental operations that might lead us to know what is true and to know and do what is good, the description and explanation of which are the business of epistemology. According to Dan Latimer, in the last phase of de Man's work there are to be found "increasingly radical meditations on the relation of language to reality."[28] But unless one has some conception of how a correct description of reality might be at least approximated to, by a suitably refined and purified language, one is in no position, as I have already argued,[29] even to make a distinction between reality and anything that language might represent. "Reality," after all, is a linguistic expression.

The direct inculcation of social norms and of "good behavior" is certainly characteristic of art or literature that is of indifferent quality and so liable to be "ideological" in the pejorative sense. Indirect influence is quite a different matter. Such evils as racial, sexual, and class prejudice always depend heavily on narrow horizons, which are imposed and kept in place largely by corrupt and slovenly uses of language. This is why good

27. See K. Wilber, ed., *Quantum Questions. Mystical Writings of the World's Great Physicists* (Boulder, Colo., and London: Shambbhala, 1984).

28. "De Man," in Irena R. Makaryk, ed., *Encyclopedia of Literary Theory* (Toronto: University of Toronto Press, 1993), 294.

29. Pp. 22, 31, 42–43 above.

literature is intrinsically subversive of them. Romantic idealizations are at best objectionable, at worst dangerous, when they are too closely attached to the ideas and assumptions that prevail in societies at any given time—as some of Rudyard Kipling's rhetoric might, by romanticizing what the British did in India, lead one to overlook some of the realities of colonial exploitation and oppression. The aesthetic is a menace when, as too often happens, it makes coercion and violence appear with "the gracefulness of a dance."[30] But it is a different matter when they rather express longing for the ideal society, probably never actually attainable in the actual circumstances of human life, in which happiness would be maximized without any sacrifice of justice,[31] and where people would always be disposed to enhance one another's lives rather than domineering over them out of cupidity, resentment, or fear.[32] And our social feelings, as opposed to our selfish inclinations and our bias on behalf of the interest groups to which we belong, do sometimes need encouragement. Certainly, it is as well not to see the state through a romantic haze. On the other hand, there remains the question of how

30. De Man, *The Rhetoric of Romanticism* (New York: Columbia University Press, 1984), 290; cited in Latimer, "De Man," 294(?).

31. The point might be illustrated by Milton's "At a Solemn Music," and the two stanzas in Marvell's "Upon Appleton House" which begin "See how the flowers as at parade." The poetry in question may have the effect described even when the reader does not share (as I actually do) the literal belief in paradise expressed both by Milton and by Marvell.

32. This ideal is approximated to by the "communist" society envisaged by Marx and perhaps explains why so insightful a critic as Terry Eagleton can continue to draw inspiration from Marxism. Schiller's *Letters on Art* stressed the organic nature of the work of art, and the harmonious balance of faculties that was the response it evoked in human consciousness. He made this a model for human relations and the conduct of society. This view is attacked by de Man as subversive of individual freedom and as apt to ratify excessive coercion by the state (Norris, *Postmodernism*, 175–76). In my view, one can appreciate the benefits of Schiller's approach, while avoiding its dangers, if one conceives the ideal society, rather than most societies as they actually are, as the proper focus of romantic idealization and longing.

individuals can envisage the collective, at least in its idealized form, with enough enthusiasm to generate the cooperation essential to civilized life.

Shelley's claim, that poets would make the best legislators, is evidently quite absurd as it stands. But it masks an insight that is of the utmost importance. Good poets "cleanse the doors of perception," enhancing our ability to experience, understand, and judge, so enabling us the better to envision what is really good, and the degree to which our individual behavior, our social systems, and our immediate political ideals fall short of it. De Man says that it is questionable whether literature gives us any information about what is other than itself.[33] The claim that it does not do so is true in one sense, false in another. According to an aesthetics that is in line with the New Enlightenment, it is not the role of literature as literature *directly* to give information or instruction; but rather it is to yield satisfaction by stimulating attentiveness and intelligence in such a way that we can ourselves judge what is true and decide what is for the best. This is why education in literature and the arts has always, and quite rightly, been assumed to be a crucial part of the upbringing of good citizens.[34] "Good citizens," of course, cannot be relied upon always to comply with whatever is demanded by authority and never to do anything that rocks the boat. On the contrary, they will be inclined to protest and to resist when ideals of justice and truth-telling are flouted by those who have the most power and influence in society.

33. *The Resistance to Theory,* 11; see Latimer, "de Man," 295.

34. De Man would resist all attempts to see the teaching of literature as a lesson in how to live properly or be a good citizen (*Resistance,* 24); he will have it that hostility to literary theory is due quite largely to its exposure of such mystifications (Latimer, "de Man," 294). He writes of the destructive effect ofthe aesthetic overstepping its proper bounds and straying into ethics, or into our beliefs about the empirical world (*Allegories of Reading* [New Haven and London: Yale University Press, 1979], 158; Latimer, loc. cit.).

CONCLUSION

ON BALANCE, the Old Enlightenment has conferred enormous benefits on humanity. But it has spawned some monsters too. One of these is "scientism," which appears to make all value an arbitrary matter, and everything specifically human illusory. Another is a limited utilitarianism that issues in consumerism; the only value that can be readily quantified is the production and consumption of goods, so it must be the only "real" value. (The step may be short, here as elsewhere, between what is tough-minded and what is merely bone-headed.) A third is a naive attitude to the darker human passions, together with the assumption that when people are shown the benefits of reason, they will always embrace it without much more ado. A fourth is an uncritical contempt for traditional ways of thinking, speaking, and acting, and a tendency to reject them before their grounds and consequences have been adequately examined.

Postmodernists tend to reject the "rationality," along with the norms of cognition and evaluation that underlie it, that seems to give rise to all these evils and is taken to be the essence of the "modern." They are apt to repudiate the related ideals of objectivity and truth as either impossible or objectionable. The constraints that these ideals appear to impose on speech and thought are accordingly surrendered in favor of either aesthetic attractiveness or anarchic freedom.

But there are many reasons, to which I have alluded repeatedly in the course of this book, for supposing that the "cure" proposed by postmodernism would be much worse than any of the diseases attributable to the Old Enlightenment. The discontents of civilization are no sufficient indication that barbarism would be preferable. Also, the unrestricted play of experience and creative intelligence, as characteristically advocated by postmodernists, so far from being hostile to reason as properly understood, is a necessary condition for its exercise. To come to judge truly about how things are in the world, it is necessary to be both as attentive and as intelligent as possible.

The Old Enlightenment never properly solved the problem of the nature and credentials of the reason it extolled; once this is done, one finds the grounds both for proper appreciation of the benefits that it has conferred and for correction of its defects and limitations as stressed by postmodernists. All four of the errors I mentioned may in principle be removed by a reason more thoroughly grounded and applied. It is less than fully reasonable to adopt a "scientism" that is in the last analysis incompatible with anyone reasonably believing it (or indeed practicing science at all); or to embrace a scheme of values so restricted as not only to starve the human spirit but to head for ecological disaster; or to fail to take into account the many aspects of human nature, whether benign or intensely dangerous, that are not readily amenable to reason; or to reject established ways of thinking and acting before their full ramifications are known, probably in deference to a "scientistic" worldview that is itself demonstrably a tissue of confusions.

Worst of all, the fashionable despair about the prospects for humankind that is fostered by postmodernism could easily prove to be a self-fulfilling prophecy. Any well-founded hope for our future must depend upon our being *more* and not *less* rational than we have been in the past. As I have been at pains to reiterate, the fundamental defect of the Old Enlightenment is not excess of rationality, but the fact that it was not quite rational enough.

BIBLIOGRAPHY

Althusser, L. *For Marx.* Harmondsworth: Penguin Books, 1969.

Aristotle. *Metaphysics.* Trans. J. Warrington. London: J. M. Dent, 1956.

———. *Politics.* Trans. T. A. Sinclair. Harmondsworth: Penguin, 1981.

———. *Posterior Analytics.* Trans. Jonathan Barnes. Oxford: Oxford University Press, 1994.

Augustine. *Contra academicos.* In *Writings of St. Augustine,* vol. 1, ed. L. Schopp. New York: Cima Publishing House, 1948.

———. *Confessions.* London: J. M. Dent, 1957.

Banks, Arthur, ed. *The Collected Papers of Charles Sanders Peirce.* Vol. VIII. Cambridge: Harvard University Press, 1958.

Bataille, Georges. *Visions of Excess. Selected Writings 1927–39.* Minneapolis: University of Minnesota Press, 1985.

Baudrillard, Jean. *La société de consommation.* Paris: Gallimard, 1970.

Bell, Daniel. *The Cultural Contradictions of Capitalism.* New York: Basic Books, 1978.

Bernstein, Richard J. *Beyond Objectivism and Relativism.* Oxford: Blackwell, 1983.

———, ed. *Habermas on Modernity.* Cambridge: Polity Press, 1985.

Blom, Eric, ed. *Grove's Dictionary of Music and Musicians.* 5th edition. London: Macmillan, 1954.

Bowlby, John. *Child Care and the Growth of Love.* Harmondsworth: Penguin Books, 1953.

Boyne, Roy. *Foucault and Derrida. The Other Side of Reason.* London: Unwin Hyman, 1990.

Calder, Nigel. *Violent Universe.* London: Futura Publications, 1975.

Casanova, José. "The Politics of the Religious Revival." *Telos,* no. 59 (Spring 1984), 3–33.

Churchland, P. *Matter and Consciousness.* Cambridge: MIT Press, 1984.

Cixous, Hélène. "The Laugh of the Medusa." In Marks and Courtivron, eds., *New French Feminisms.*

———. "Sorties." In Betsy Wing, ed., *The Newly Born Woman.*

Clastres, Pierre. *Recherches d'anthropologie politique.* Paris: Seuil, 1980.

Coleridge, S. T. *Biographia Literaria.* London: J. M. Dent, 1956.
Courtivron, Isabelle de. *See* Marks, Elaine.
Culler, Jonathan. *On Deconstruction. Theory and Criticism after Structuralism.* Ithaca, N.Y.: Cornell University Press, 1982.
Dancy, Jonathan. *Contemporary Epistemology.* Oxford: Blackwell, 1985.
De Bono, Edward. *Lateral Thinking.* New York: Harper and Row, 1973.
De Man, Paul. *Allegories of Reading.* New Haven and London: Yale University Press, 1979.
———. *The Rhetoric of Romanticism.* New York: Columbia University Press, 1984.
———. *The Resistance to Theory.* Minneapolis: University of Minnesota Press, 1986.
Derrida, Jacques. *Speech and Phenomena: And Other Essays on Husserl's Theory of Signs.* Evanston: Northwestern University Press, 1973.
———. *Of Grammatology.* Baltimore: Johns Hopkins University Press, 1976.
———. *Limited Inc.* Baltimore: John Hopkins University Press, 1977.
———. *Language, Counter-Memory, Practice.* Oxford: Blackwell, 1977.
———. *Writing and Difference.* Chicago: University of Chicago Press, 1978.
———. *Positions.* Chicago: University of Chicago Press, 1981.
———. *Dissemination.* London: Athlone Press, 1981.
———. *Margins of Philosophy.* Chicago: University of Chicago Press, 1982.
———. *Glas.* Lincoln, Nebr.: University of Nebraska Press, 1986.
———. *The Post Card. From Socrates to Freud and Beyond.* Trans. Alan Bass. Chicago: University of Chicago Press, 1987.
———, ed. (with Mustapha Tilli). *For Nelson Mandela.* New York: Seaver, 1987.
———. "Like the sound of the sea deep within a shell: Paul de Man's War." *Critical Inquiry* 14 (Spring 1988), 590–652.
———. *Points . . . Interviews, 1974–1994.* Stanford, Calif.: Stanford University Press, 1995.
Descartes, René. *Meditations on First Philosophy.* In E. Anscombe and P.T. Geach, eds., *Descartes. Selected Writings.* Edinburgh: Nelson, 1954.
Drury, Shadia B. *Alexander Kojève: The Roots of Post-Modernism.* New York: St. Martin's Press, 1994.
Duchen, Claire. *Feminism in France: From May '68 to Mitterand.* London: Routledge and Kegan Paul, 1986.
Eccles, D. *See* Popper, K. R.

Ellis, John. *Against Deconstruction.* Princeton: Princeton University Press, 1989.

Farrell, Warren. *The Myth of Male Power.* New York: Simon and Schuster, 1993.

Feyerabend, Paul. "Consolations for the Specialist." In Lakatos and Musgrave, *Criticism.*

Foucault, Michel. *Madness and Civilization. A History of Insanity in the Age of Reason.* London: Tavistock, 1971.

———. *Discipline and Punish.* New York: Vintage Press, 1975.

———. *Language, Counter-Memory, Practice.* Ithaca, N.Y.: Cornell University Press, 1977.

———. *The History of Sexuality.* New York: Random House, 1978.

———. *The Use of Pleasure.* Harmondsworth: Penguin Books, 1986.

———. *Power/Knowledge.* New York: Pantheon Books, 1987.

———. *Politics, Philosophy, Culture.* New York: Routledge, 1988.

Frankel, Boris. "The Cultural Contradictions of Postmodernity." In Milner, *Postmodern.*

Fraser, Nancy. "Foucault on Modern Power: Empirical Insights and Normative Confusions." *Praxis International* 1, no. 3 (October 1981).

French, Marilyn. *Beyond Power. On Women, Men and Morals.* New York: Summit Books, 1985.

Freud, S. *Beyond the Pleasure Principle.* New York: Norton, 1990.

———. *Civilization and Its Discontents.* London: Hogarth Press, 1930.

———. *New Introductory Lectures on Psychoanalysis.* New York: Norton, 1990.

Fry, Roger. *Vision and Design.* Harmondsworth: Penguin Books, 1960.

Gates, Henry Louis, Jr., ed. *Race, Writing and Difference.* Chicago and London: University of Chicago Press, 1986.

Gettier, Edmund. "Is Justified True Belief Knowledge?" *Analysis* 23, no. 6 (June 1963), 121–23.

Guattari, F. "The Postmodern Dead End." *Flash Art* 28 (May/June 1986), 41–56.

Handy, Charles. *The Age of Paradox.* Cambridge, Mass.: Harvard Business School Press, 1994.

Hesse, Mary. *Revolutions and Reconstructions in the Philosophy of Science.* Bloomington: Indiana University Press, 1980.

Hollingdale, R. J. "Introduction" to Friedrich Nietzsche, *Thus Spake Zarathustra.* Harmondsworth: Penguin Books, 1969.

Horton, Robin. "African Traditional Thought and Western Science." In Bryan Wilson, ed., *Rationality.* Oxford: Blackwell, 1970.

Hume, David. *An Enquiry Concerning Human Understanding.* Oxford: Clarendon Press, 1957.

Irigaray, Luce. *The Sex Which Is Not One.* Ithaca, N.Y.: Cornell University Press, 1985.

Jennings, P. *The Jenguin Pennings.* Harmondsworth: Penguin Books, 1963.

Jung, C. G. *Psychological Types.* London: Kegan Paul, 1923.

Kamuf, Peggy, ed. *A Derrida Reader. Between the Blinds.* New York: Columbia University Press, 1991.

Kant, Immanuel. *Critique of Pure Reason.* London: Macmillan, 1933.

Kaufmann, Walter. *Nietzsche. Philosopher, Psychologist, Antichrist.* Cleveland and New York: World Publishing Company, 1956.

Keirsey, David, and Marilyn Bates. *Please Understand Me. Character and Temperamental.* Del Mar, Calif.: Prometheus Nemesis, 1984.

Koertge, Noretta. *See* Patai, Daphne.

Kolb, David. *Postmodern Sophistications.* Chicago and London: University of Chicago Press, 1990.

Kristeva, Julia. *About Chinese Women.* New York: Urizen Books, 1974.

———. *Desire in Language.* New York: Columbia University Press, 1982.

———. *Powers of Horror.* New York: Columbia University Press, 1982.

———. *Revolution in Poetic Languages.* New York: Columbia University Press, 1984.

Kritzman, L. D., ed. *Politics, Philosophy and Culture.* London: Routledge and Kegan Paul, 1988.

Kroker, A., and D. Cook. *The Postmodern Scene. Excremental Culture and Hyper-Aesthetics.* Montreal: New World Perspectives, 1986.

Laing, R. D. (with Aaron Esterson). *The Families of Schizophrenics.* London: Tavistock Publications, 1964.

———. *The Divided Self.* Harmondsworth: Penguin Books, 1965.

Lakatos, I., with A. Musgrave, eds. *Criticism and the Growth of Knowledge.* Cambridge: Cambridge University Press, 1970.

Larson, Peter. "Modern Life Spawns Pradoxes." *Calgary Herald,* December 31 1994.

Latimer, Dan. "De Man." In Makaryk, Irene R., *Encyclopedia.*

Lawson, H. *Reflexivity: The Postmodern Predicament.* London: Hutchinson, 1985.

Lewis, C. S. *Undeceptions.* London: Geoffrey Bles, 1971.

Lonergan, B. J. F. *Insight. A Study of Human Understanding.* Toronto: University of Toronto Press, 1992.

———. *Method in Theology.* London: Darton, Longman and Todd, 1971.

Lyons, W. "Modern Work on Intentionality." In J. J. MacIntosh and H. A. Meynell, eds., *Faith, Scepticism, and Personal Identity.* Calgary: University of Calgary Press, 1994.

Lyotard, J.-F. *Dérivé à partir de Marx et Freud.* Paris: 10/18 UGE, 1973.

———. *The Postmodern Condition.* Minneapolis: University of Minnesota Press, 1984.

———. *Just Gaming.* Minneapolis: University of Minnesota Press, 1985.

———. *La Faculté de Juger.* Paris: Editions de Minuit, 1985.

———. "Rules and Paradoxes and Svelte Appendix." *Cultural Critique,* 1986.

———. *Le Postmoderne expliqué aux enfants.* Paris: Galilee, 1986.

———. *The Différend: Phrases in Dispute.* Minneapolis: University of Minnesota Press, 1988.

Makaryk, Irene R., ed. *Encyclopedia of Literary Theory.* Toronto: University of Toronto Press, 1993.

Marks, Elaine, and Isabelle de Courtivron, eds. *New French Feminisms.* New York: Schocken Books, 1981.

Mason, Jeff, and Peter Washington. *The Future of Thinking. Rhetoric and Liberal Arts Teaching.* London: Routledge, 1992.

McLellan, D. *The Thought of Karl Marx. An Introduction.* London: Macmillan, 1971.

Meynell, Hugo A. *Freud, Marx and Morals.* New York: Barnes and Noble, 1981.

———. *The Intelligible Universe. A Cosmological Argument.* New York: Barnes and Noble, 1982.

———. *The Nature of Aesthetic Value.* Albany: State University of New York Press, 1986.

———. *An Introduction to the Philosophy of Bernard Lonergan.* Toronto: University of Toronto Press, 1992.

———. "Lonergan's Cognitional Theory and Method in Psychology." *Theory in Psychology* 4, no. 2 (1994), 53–68.

———. "On Nietzsche, Postmodernism and the New Enlightenment." *New Blackfriars* 76, no. 889 (January 1995), 4–18.

———. *Redirecting Philosophy.* Toronto: University of Toronto Press, 1998.

Michelson, Annette. "Heterology and the Critique of Instrumental Reason." *October* (Spring 1986), 125–26.

Mill, J. S. *Utilitarianism.* London: J. M. Dent, 1964.

Milne, A. A. *The House at Pooh Corner.* Toronto: McClelland and Stewart, 1925.

Milner, Andrew, et al., eds. *Postmodern Conditions.* Oxford and Providence, R.I.: Berg Publishers, 1990.

Moi, Toril. *Sexual/Textual Politics. Feminist Literary Theory.* New York: Methuen, 1985.

Monod, Jacques. *Chance and Necessity.* London: Collins, 1972.

Moore, G. E. *Principia Ethica.* Cambridge: Cambridge University Press, 1956.

———. *Philosophical Papers.* London: Allen and Unwin, 1959.

Morison, Samuel Eliot. *The Oxford History of the American People.* New York: Oxford University Press, 1965.

Newman, J. H. *An Essay on the Development of Christian Doctrine.* London: Longmans, Green and Co., 1890.

Nietzsche, Friedrich. *The Gay Science.* New York: Random House, 1974.

———. *Thus Spoke Zarathustra.* Translated by Walter Kaufmann. Harmondsworth: Penguin Books, 1978.

———. *The Antichrist* and *Ecce Homo.* New York: Random House, 1989.

———. *Beyond Good and Evil.* Buffalo, N.Y.: Prometheus Books, 1989.

Norris, Christopher. "Deconstruction, Postmodernism and Philosophy: Habermas on Derrida." In Wood, *Derrida.*

———. *The Truth about Postmodernism.* Oxford: Blackwells, 1993.

Novak, Michael. *The Spirit of Democratic Capitalism.* New York: Simon and Schuster, 1982.

Orenstein, A. *Willard Van Orman Quine.* Boston: Twayne Publications, 1977.

Paglia, Camille. *Sexual Personae.* New York: Random House, 1991.

Pascal, Blaise. *Pensées.* Harmondsworth: Penguin Books, 1966.

Patai, Daphne, and Noretta Koertge. *Professing Feminism. Cautionary Tales from the Strange World of Women's Studies.* New York: Basic Books, 1994.

Pefanis, Julian. *Heterology and the Postmodern. Bataille, Baudrillard and Lyotard.* Durham, N.C., and London: Duke University Press, 1991.

Peirce, C. S. *Collected Papers,* vol. VIII. Edited by Arthur Banks. Cambridge: Harvard University Press, 1958.

Percesepe, Gary John. *Future(s) of Philosophy. The Marginal Thinking of Jacques Derrida.* New York: Peter Lang, 1989.

Pitcher, George, ed. *Wittgenstein. The Philosophical Investigations.* London: Macmillans, 1968.

Plato. *The Republic.* Trans. H. D. P. Lee. Harmondsworth: Penguin Books, 1955.

———. *Phaedrus.* Trans. Reginald Hackforth. Cambridge: Cambridge University Press, 1972.

———. *Meno.* Trans. R. W. Sharples. Oakville, Conn.: David Brown, 1985.

Popper, K. R. *Objective Knowledge. An Evolutionary Approach.* Oxford: Clarendon Press, 1972.

———. (with D. Eccles). *The Self and Its Brain.* Berlin: Springer, 1977.

Potter, Stephen. *One-upmanship.* New York: Holt, 1955.

Potter, Vincent G. *Charles S. Peirce on Norms and Ideals.* Worcester, Mass.: University of Massachusetts Press, 1967.

Putnam, Hilary. *Rationality with a Human Face.* Cambridge, Mass.: Harvard University Press, 1981.

———. *Renewing Philosophy.* Cambridge, Mass.: Harvard University Press, 1992.

Rorty, Richard. *Philosophy and the Mirror of Nature.* Princeton: Princeton University Press, 1979.

———. "Habermas and Lyotard on Postmodernism." In Bernstein, *Habermas.*

Russell, Bertrand. *A History of Western Philosophy.* London: Allen and Unwin, 1946.

Sellars, Wilfred. *Science, Perception and Reality.* London: Routledge and Kegan Paul, 1963.

Sennett, Richard. *The Fall of Public Man.* Cambridge: Cambridge University Press, 1977.

Skinner, B. F. *Science and Human Behavior.* New York: Free Press, 1953.

———. *Beyond Freedom and Dignity.* London: Jonathan Cape, 1972.

Sommers, Christina Hoff. *Who Stole Feminism?* New York: Simon and Schuster, 1994.

Symons, Donald. *The Evolution of Human Sexuality.* Oxford: Oxford University Press, 1979.

Taylor, A. E. *Plato. The Man and His Work.* London: Methuen, 1960.

Taylor, Gordon Rattray. *Sex in History.* London: Thames and Hudson, 1954.

Toffler, Alvin. *The Third Wave.* London: Pan Books, 1980.

Tong, Rosemarie. *Feminist Thought.* Boulder, Colo., and San Francisco: Westview Press, 1989.

Wenzel, H. V. "The Text as Body/Politics." *Feminist Studies* 7, no. 2 (Summer 1981): 264–87.

White, Nicholas B. *Plato on Knowledge and Reality.* Indianapolis: Hackett Publishing Co., 1976.

Wilber, Ken, ed. *Quantum Questions. Mystical Writings of the World's Great Physicists.* Boulder, Colo., and London: Shambhala Press, 1984.

Williams, Bernard. *Ethics and the Limits of Philosophy.* Cambridge: Harvard University Press, 1985.

Williams, M. E. *Groundless Belief.* Oxford: Oxford University Press, 1977.

Wing, Betsy, ed. *The Newly Born Woman.* Minneapolis: University of Minnesota Press, 1986.

Wittgenstein, L. *Tractatus Logico-Philosophicus.* London: Routledge and Kegan Paul, 1961.

———. *Philosophical Investigations.* Oxford: Blackwell, 1958.

———. *On Certainty.* Oxford: Blackwell, 1969.

Wood, David, ed. *Derrida. A Critical Reader.* Oxford: Blackwells 1992.

Worsthorne, Peregrine."Our Current Problems." *Encounter.* Vol. LII, no. 4 (April 1979), 12–13.

INDEX

Postmodernism and the New Enlightenment was composed in Adobe Garamond
by WorldComp, Sterling, Virgina; printed on 60-pound Writers Natural and
bound by McNaughton & Gunn Lithographers, Saline, Michigan; and
designed and produced by Kachergis Book Design,
Pittsboro, North Carolina.